MW00881466

A Way Up
Hope and Help for Teen Boys and Young Men

Angie Dent

Other Books by Angie Dent

- A Way Up **2**
  Hope and Help for Teen Girls
  and Young Women

- Poetry Like Chocolate

- Food for the Soul: A Christian Experience

- Food for the Soul:
  A Journal for More Happiness

- Just for Girlfriends!! 2

- Just for Girlfriends!!

- FINISH: 28 Declarations to
  Move You One Step Closer to
  Your Dream

- FINISH JOURNAL: A Guide to Move You
  Closer to Your Dream

- Covenant Keeper:
  Poetic Stories of God's Promises
  to Every Believer

- Covenant Keeper 2:
  Stories of God's Promises to
  Every Believer

- Cumplidor del Pacto –
  Historias Poéticas de las Promesas de Dios
  para Cada Creyente

A Way Up

Hope and Help for Teen Boys and Young Men

Angie Dent

Acknowledgements

This book would not have been possible without help from God and many kind people. God's many blessings to all.

Give a Man a Fish and You Feed Him for a Day. Teach Him How to Fish and You Feed Him for a Lifetime.

Chinese philosopher Lao Tzu

CONTENTS

INTRODUCTION

We all need a helping hand every now and then. This book gives you hands of help and hope. You'll find new beginnings and many reasons to get up in the morning.

Fresh start. Right now. That's what you're being offered in this book. Right here is hope. Right here is a way up. Right here is a way out of your situation.

If you're a teen boy or a young man tired of struggling with unemployment, education, need a second chance, or want a better life, this book will help you.

Parents, grandparents, aunts, uncles, cousins, and families, this book is for you too. This is a book of possibilities. Inside are answers, help, and support that you've been searching for to help your teen boys and young men.

A Way Up was written to help lessen the cycle of unemployment, offer a second chance, help improve in school, get a GED, go to college, and improve daily living.

You will find helpful resources, important information, and words that lift you higher. You will see many reasons to keep trying and not give up.

Inside are valuable tools, support, and guidance that will give you confidence to step out and improve your today and future. You will be inspired, while being pointed in the right direction.

You will be helped to start dreaming and see yourself beyond where you are right now. You will discover and unlock abilities and dreams that you never knew were there. You will learn how to make those dreams a reality, for a better today and a brighter future.

You will be shown how to:
- *Get and keep a job*
- *Make a second chance count*
- *See the best in you*
- *Be positive toward yourself*
- *Get the most out of your money*
- *Plan for and go to college*
- *Get a GED and make it work for you*
- *Discover and go after your dreams*

I hope A Way Up will help you become the best that you can be. As you read these pages, be open to receiving information given. I'm confident that by taking these steps and using the information shared, you will get help that could change the rest of your life. I believe you will like the change.

CHAPTER ONE
We See You

You have abilities. You have talents. You have skills.

Before now, maybe you didn't think you had choices. Or, perhaps you didn't see a future because you made some poor decisions or mistakes. There isn't a person alive who hasn't made mistakes. We can't do anything about the past, but we can learn from it and do better. We can start by creating a brighter future right where we are.

You can have a better now. Having better is within reach. If you want it, it's yours. The first step to get there is to know that you're not invisible. There are crowds of people who see you.

There are people in many places willing to help. They can help, if you let them. Your future matters. How and where you end up in life matters. You have talents that you think no one sees. People see.

We see you holding paint brushes splashing red, yellow, and green on walls and paper, drawing pictures of your life, telling your story. Such amazing talent is wrapped up in your hands. That tiny treasure can make huge changes in your life!

We see you throwing a basketball, shot after shot swooshing clean through the net. That wonderful skill can take you places!

We know these are just a few things you're good at and can do. You have abilities. You have talents. You have skills. They can be put to use in so many different, amazing ways.

Your talents can take you places that you never even dreamed of. Start using your talents. Let them be seen. Work hard to improve them. Do your very best. If you use them, you can win.

Don't let your circumstances stop you from becoming who and what you can be. No matter what has happened or is happening where you are, don't give up. Keep looking for better. Circumstances can't break you unless you let them. You can overcome your current situation. You were made for more.

Kevin (not his real name) lived with his mom and sisters. In his neighborhood, all through the day, men stood on corners and leaned into cars selling drugs. Kevin kept his head down and stayed away from that. Most times he worked small jobs, to help his mom pay rent. He was even trying to get his GED, to get a steady job.

One afternoon, while he was home alone, a car drove by. Someone from inside started shooting into Kevin's house. He was shot over 6 times. He was only 22.

The family later heard, what they already knew, the shooter had the wrong house. The miraculous thing was that Kevin survived. Bullets missed his heart and head.

While recovering, he told his family that, he didn't remember how he got out of the house. All he was thinking was, he wanted to live. If he got outside, somebody could help him live.

After the shooting, Kevin could have stopped trying to get his GED. He could have easily quit. Without a doubt, being shot changed his life and his families'. Having to go through surgeries and physical therapy were very hard times.

After full recovery, he got his GED. It took a while, but he got it. That led to a full-time permanent job. Right now, he's still working and living in a different, better place.

Countless men who were in similar situations as Kevin, and you, now live a better life. Their situations were different, but their stories were all the same. They grew up in your neighborhoods. They went to your schools. They walked in your shoes. They were your story. They lived it.

They were surrounded by the same choices and things that you're surrounded by, but they chose to not give up. They found out that people did see them. People did see the good in them. They discovered the good in themselves too. Maybe words from a kind teacher, a friend's parent, a preacher, or an encouraging book opened their eyes.

Today, they are doctors, pharmacists, judges, chefs, business owners, social workers, teachers, professional athletes and many other titles. How did they get that way? How did they get to where they are now? I'm glad you asked. They got there through confidence and hard work.

They chose to make better choices. They stayed in the race of life. They stayed in school. Some went back to school. Others even made second chances count. They worked hard to get a better life. The same thing can happen to and for you. You're not less than. You can follow in their footsteps.

Right now, maybe you can't see yourself having a better life like them, because you dropped out of school. Yes, in order to do what those men did, education will be needed. But, it's not impossible. You still have plenty hope.

There are companies and people available that provide job training, job search help, GED classes, math and reading tutoring, interview practice. All of it is free. All of it was created to help people just like you. Why? Because, people see you.

You control the doorway to your future. You're probably thinking it's not that easy to just start. Right now, it may not seem easy. All it really takes is the decision to just do it. After deciding, start doing it. Give it a try. Your way isn't working out. Come at it another way.

Not having an education only leads to unnecessary frustrations. Everything in life is tied to it. By giving it a try, you will have more and better choices. Life will be less stressful. A whole new world will open up for you.

Getting tutoring and your GED can take an enormous amount of pressure off you. It'll feel like a ton of bricks was lifted off your shoulders. It can make your life a lot easier.

Without it, you're tying your own hands. Why not choose to get it and free yourself? Once you have education, it's yours. You own it. No one can take it away from you. Do your part and don't give it away.

The saying, knowledge is power, is true and powerful. Once you have knowledge from education, you choose where and how high you want to go in life. That's power. Once you get it, a whole new world will open up for you. You will discover how smart you really are. You will see how easy it is for you to learn and create good things.

There will be more chances for jobs that pay more money. You can go from walking or taking a bus to owning a car. Your family can go from renting an apartment to eventually owning a house.

If you've been bringing someone along to help you with job applications and important forms, that can stop. You will gain confidence to take care of those things easier and faster, by yourself.

If you've been having trouble understanding information or explaining written information to people, it'll help with that too. You will see how much better you will be able to explain things and be understood, the way you want.

If taking the written test to get a driver's license is holding you back, you can get confidence to take care of that too. Even without owning a car yet, you will be glad that you were able to take the test.

Getting these things would only be the beginning. You could have so much more. Don't let what happened or didn't work out stop you from becoming who and what you can become.

You have to say to yourself, this is worth my hard work. This is worth getting up early in the morning to do. This is worth staying up late to learn. High school education has great value.

The value of having it is greater than the cost of taking time to get it. The benefits are waiting for you. Why not give education another chance?

You have abilities. You have talents. You have skills. You can learn anything. Change won't happen tomorrow. It'll take time. Take it day by day. Stick with it and you will see results. Just take one step forward. What do you have to lose?

CHAPTER TWO
You Can

You have to see the best in you.

You have to believe that you can get out of situations holding you back. Circumstances can only improve if there are beliefs that improvements are possible. Being able to see a better future is very important. It starts with believing better about yourself.

Michael (not his real name) and his five brothers and sisters lived with their parents in the projects. His daddy and mama worked, but some months, light and phone bills couldn't be paid. Neither one of them finished high school. But, it didn't stop them from making sure their kids stayed in school and out of trouble.

Michael's dad stayed on his case about not doing anything. He said that he and the rest of his children shouldn't be wasting time by doing nothing. Doing nothing always led to trouble.

Michael was smart and did well in school. He also liked to draw. He used books and drawing to not waste time. He drew on paper, books, sidewalks, and everything else.

After a while, his teacher started to notice his talent. One day, she asked to look at his drawings. He showed her a picture of his courtyard.

A thin bent over man was smoking a long, brown cigarette and leaning against a rusty rail. Women with colored scarves tied on their heads stood behind plastic chairs, combing little girls' hair. Scattered trash, needles, and beer bottles rested atop patches of dirt. A child's lost sock lay beside a skinny tree with a few green leaves.

She liked his work and told him so. She started bringing him books with pictures of new, huge buildings with sparkly lights and big, pretty houses. She told him he could draw those too. In time, he started to believe her. He told his daddy what she said and showed him the books and new drawings. His daddy said that drawing could get him out of the projects.

When in high school, Michael heard how joining the army could pay for college. After graduation, he joined. When he got out, he went to college. For 30 years Michael worked in an office as an architect, drawing designs of tall buildings and houses while managing people.

How you see yourself and what you think about you matter. You have to believe in yourself. Someone once said that success starts in the mind. Man succeeds because he thinks he can. Man fails because he believes he will.

We have to pay attention to the words we speak about ourselves. When we're not aware of our words, we could easily talk ourselves out of better. What we say to and about ourselves while working toward better determines when and if we get there. You have to see the best in you.

Don't be against you. Start being for you. Say positive things. You won't go up if you're always tearing yourself down. You choose what you say, think, and dwell on. Why not say something of value about you. We all have value. Don't settle for less. Don't put up limits.

If needed, write down the good things about you. If they're written down, look at those words every day and say them to yourself. When you look at the good, you will start to notice different, better things.

Suppose someone was leaving a store at night and dropped $100.00? Without noticing, all night, people passed by and walked on top of it. Some even crushed it under wet, heavy boots. In the morning, the dirty and torn money could be seen laying on the ground. If you were the first person to see it, would you still want that money? Would you walk past it and not bother to pick it up? What happened to that money didn't change its worth. The value didn't suddenly drop to $20.00, $10.00 or $1.00. That $100.00 value was still there.

Just like that money, all of us have had things happen to us in life. Those things don't determine who we are and what we can become. They don't change our worth. We still have value, no matter what.

See your worth. See your value. See yourself the way you want to be seen. If you want people to see you in a positive, good way, you have to see yourself that way.

While moving toward better, old habits of negative thoughts will come. Each time they show up, replace them with something good and positive. Staying confident is necessary.

Those old, negative words and thoughts will come to try and make you give up hope. They'll show up to steal that better future. Be ready. Get ready ahead of time so you won't quit and give up.

When negative thoughts come, be ready to replace them with at least 2 or 3 "I can's". I can learn anything. I can have a better life. I can win. If you're always saying negative things about yourself, it's a habit. Because it's a habit, negative words will automatically come when progress is slow or when something bad happens. That old habit will have to be replaced with a new, better one.

All through the day, keep saying positive words. Be committed. Stick with it. The more positive words are spoken, the greater your confidence will be. Speaking positive words for a good future will keep discouragement away. It will also help to improve in many areas.

Equally important, we have to be careful about the words we receive from other people. Without realizing, some people push down others by speaking negative words to or about them. If those words aren't ignored, we will start to believe them. We're not what people call us. We're what we answer to. What we answer to comes from how we see ourselves and what we think about us. We don't have to listen to negativity.

We turn negative words around by ignoring negative talk and speaking good, positive words about us. When we do, we pull ourselves up. That's how we keep healthy self-esteem. That's how we start to change our future. Our confidence gets stronger and we can keep going.

All the positive words and encouragement can be said, but it's really what you say about you that matters. It's what you say about you that'll bring better. Winning begins in the mind. If you don't think you can do something, you won't. You have to believe better about you in order to make those first little steps that lead to big, better changes. If steps are taken, you will have a newness on the inside. That'll produce change on the outside.

This isn't just about speaking positive words. This is about speaking good words about you and believing it. It's up to you to do your part. If you keep saying good things, not much will happen. A shift won't be there. But, if you keep saying good things about yourself and start believing those things, something will happen. Something good will happen.

The picture that you have about you will start to look different. You will begin to see yourself, circumstances, situations, and life differently.

A boost of confidence and hope will be there. You will see yourself better and will want better. In the end, you will have better, because you'll start to move toward it.

When we know who we are on the inside, we don't have to prove we're important on the outside. We don't have to keep trying to prove we're good enough.

When we build ourselves up with positive words, we see we're good enough. We see our worth.

Ask yourself this question and think about how to answer. What do I like most about me? Write it down and put a date on it. Months later or even a year later, ask yourself that same question. See if you have the same answer or a better one.

Positive Affirmations

- I can be successful

- I can learn anything

- I can do anything I set my mind to

- I have value

- I am worth something

- I have what it takes to win

- I am important to me

- I am talented

- I am somebody

- I believe in me

- I am a winner

- I choose to not give up

- Quitting is not an option

- I will be successful

CHAPTER THREE
Unlock Your Dreams

You can become what you dream.

A dream is a serious want or hope to get or achieve something specific.

This chapter shows the power of dreams and goals. It unlocks the possibilities that begin with dreams and continue through goals. You'll see how to turn your dreams into reality.

A bright future is yours for the taking. You can have it, if you start dreaming. Dreams help you see the impossible. They help you to believe that better is possible. You can be whatever you want to be. Just dream. Stretch your imagination. Start dreaming. You can become what you dream.

To start your dream, find out what you're really good at. It's usually something you can do well with little or no effort. Suppose you find yourself cooking all the time. You enjoy it and can't get away from it. People love the taste of your food. Family and friends can't wait to sit at the table to eat barbecue chicken and ribs cooked in your thick home-made sauce. After dinner, plates are always empty. The only thing left are bones and thin, red streaks, where people dragged their fingers scraping up every drop of that delicious sauce.

If people react that way or similarly to your food, turn that into your dream. It's possible to make a very good living in the food industry. You could start as a prep cook, getting seasonings and small foods ready for the chef. From there, you could move up to higher cook positions. If you're learning about food and business the whole time you're working, you could even end up as kitchen manager or executive chef.

Cooking shows are great examples of people creating dreams and working hard to get them. There are cooking competitions with prize money from $10,000.00 up to $100,000.00. On Chopped, a Food Network adult competition, a man from New Orleans competed and won. To get there, he beat out many top home cooks and chefs from around the world. In that one-hour competition, he won $10,000.00. You couldn't wipe that big smile off his face. He started doing the happy dance and saying 10 stacks. Ten stacks. Wouldn't it be nice for that to be you? Well, you see that it can be done. You won't start at his dollar level. You'll have to start smaller and work your way up. But, you can do it.

On Chopped Junior, the little kids also compete for $10,000.00. On Master Chef Junior kids compete for even greater prize money. They have kids as young as 8 years old competing for prize money of $100,000.00. Yes, that's right. Eight years old. Yes, I said one hundred thousand dollars. In those weeks-long competitions, kids end up learning from some of the best chefs in the world. Imagine that. If those young children can do it, you can too. Don't let a bunch of little kids beat you!

Starting small can still make money. It'll also give you time to learn more and build confidence. Test it out. If family and friends like your food, try co-workers. From there, try friends of family and friends.

If your food tastes good and is presented professionally, the word will get out. People will buy it. They'll start recommending it to others.

You don't have to stop there. See how far you can go. Work your way up to farmer's markets, local festivals, out-of-town events, small and large cooking competitions, small and large catering for businesses, organizations, churches. Who knows? Maybe one day you could even have your own food truck, franchise, restaurant, on line cooking show, or write a cookbook.

Maybe you're not into cooking. That's okay. We all have different likes and talents. Maybe you like to work on machines or cars. Being interested in any one of those things could be a dream too.

If you like working on machines, becoming a **mechanical engineer** could be your dream. You'd be doing something you like and making a good living. Mechanical engineers are well paid. They make a lot of money operating and fixing machines for air conditioners and heating. They work in hotels, restaurants, buildings, businesses, and homes. You could start off as an apprentice, learning from an experienced engineer. From there, move up to engineer or eventually senior engineer.

Electrical engineering is another option. As an **electrical engineer** you'd be installing, fixing, and taking care of electrical wiring and equipment. Every business and home need lights. You could definitely make a good living. You'd start as an apprentice there too, but could learn and move up. That's another skill that you could eventually use to open your own business.

Maybe you're always working under the hood of a car. If fixing cars is your talent, becoming a **mechanic** could be your dream. If you've ever brought a car to be repaired, you know mechanics make a good living. The amount they charge to fix cars isn't cheap. You could start working in the service department at a car dealership or other repair shop. Also, most oil change businesses make car repairs. From there, you could eventually move up and someday own your own repair shop.

Even if you just like driving, that could be a dream. **Truck drivers** make a good living. Some drive for department stores and companies. Others drive for companies a while before saving up money to buy their own trucks. They then start their own businesses. Some even buy tow trucks and tow cars for insurance companies and people.

If numbers are the only things that keep your attention, turn that into your dream. There are plenty well-paying jobs that use different types of math. **Structural engineers** use math to help build bridges, buildings, and structures based on weight. Mechanical engineers also use some math. **Accountants** use math to keep up with million-dollar budgets for businesses and people. You could also be a math **teacher** or **college professor.**

If drawing and creating is your thing, you have plenty options to start your dream. **Artists**, **graphic designers**, **architects**, **interior designers** use drawing to create paintings, computer images, blue prints for houses and buildings.

If you're drawn to science, maybe a **doctor**, **chemist**, **scientist** or a **pharmacist** could be your dream.

If you want to try hands-on learning in science, technology, engineering, and math, there's a non-profit business in New Orleans that offers a monthly program a few hours on Saturdays. STEM NOLA has a program for students up to 12th grade who are interested in learning more about science, technology, engineering, and math (STEM).

Students are welcome to learn and participate in free project-based activities and hands-on training taught by STEM college students, business volunteers and mentors. Contact them at info@stemnola.com, www.stemnola.com, or (504) 391-0730 for full information.

Perhaps you like to exercise. Becoming a personal trainer or physical therapist could be your dream. As a **personal trainer**, you get to work out with clients, while getting paid. You'd be doing something you love and helping people get healthy. You could start by working at a gym. After gaining experience, you could eventually move up to having your own business.

There are personal trainers who have on-line businesses, their own studio, or train at client's homes or offices. You would be responsible for getting and keeping your own clients, setting your own hours and pricing.

Most personal trainers with their own businesses get started with just a 3-month certification.

If you enjoy exercising, having a dream of becoming a **physical therapist** is another option. Instead of exercising with people, you'd be helping them recover from injuries, through use of mild exercise and stretching. You could start as a physical therapist aide or technician, working at clinics, hospitals, and private practices.

Being an aide or technician would help with learning about being a physical therapist. From there, you could prepare to work as a physical therapist assistant. There are 2-year college programs for assistants and 4-year college programs for physical therapists. Both are good careers and pay well.

You don't have to stay there. There are stages for physical therapists. Some are even doctors of physical therapy. This is a career that you could also eventually start your own business.

What if you like to build and fix things? Jobs in **construction** could be your dream. There is good pay there too. You could work and learn about building houses, office spaces, backyard decks, home repairs, wood work. Maybe one day, you could build your own house for your family.

Maybe your dream is to play football, basketball or other sport. If your talent lands you a college scholarship, great! Congratulations! While there, make that free education work for you. Select a major that will help you after college. Study like the cost for college is coming out of your own pocket.

Getting and keeping education gives you permission to succeed. If you get hurt or something happens and you can't play that sport anymore, you would have a backup plan. You would have choices. You would have a Plan B, Plan C, and all the way through Z.

Here's something else that will help. Take time to listen to before and after game interviews by your favorite player. Pay attention to how he explains himself. He may have gotten where he is by playing football or whatever the sport, but he also used education, hard work, and discipline. Working at all of those things helped him explain himself well, understand contracts, get better endorsements and other opportunities to professionally represent the companies. Afterall, they are paying him to wear their products and talk about them. He has to do a good job to keep representing them.

There are some dreams that you can get training for in 3 months, 6 months, 9 months, 2 years, 4 years, or more.

Whatever your dream ends up being, you'll still need a high school education. Everything mentioned here will require a high school education. As shared in a previous chapter, everything really does rely on education. Having a high school education is needed for daily living. Using every day basic math, reading, and English are needed for every job, not just special dreams.

If you're still in school, but struggling, stay in school. Do your best. Keep at it. If you're having trouble learning, talk to your teacher or any teacher. Tell him or her that you want to do better. That person would likely be more than happy and willing to help.

Don't worry about what friends or other people might think. It's more important what you think about you. Focus on getting what you need to make a better you and a better future. Don't let what people might think rob you of future money, your future car, house, or choice of living anywhere you want.

Do your best and get your grades up. Look at the list of dream options given right here. Basic information has been provided. Take the next step and find out more about these jobs and how much they pay. Choose one. Start dreaming about going to college or getting a certificate. Visit college websites and see what interests you.

Maybe you just want a better life. You're doing well in school and your dream is to go to college. But, your family can't afford it. First off, good job at doing well in school!

Keep up the good work! You're on the right track. Stay there. Keep doing well in school and stay focused. Don't worry about what some people may say, because you like school. You're going somewhere. You could go to college, get a good job and be the one in charge.

Those same people who were calling you names for doing well could one day be asking you for a job. They could be calling you a new name, Boss.

Now, start dreaming. Decide what you want to be. There's a lot of information and ideas right here, to get started.

After choosing a career, start looking at college websites to see what classes are offered for the career you chose. Get tuition, information on college life, and other things they have to offer. Set up an in-person tour, to see up close.

While still in school, keep your grades up. Focus on raising your GPA. There are academic scholarships available to students with excellent grades. Don't wait for your school's guidance counselor to talk to you about scholarship opportunities. Let him or her know you're interested in them. He or she will take it from there. After about a month or two, check back with the counselor and see what your options are.

If you're a high school junior or senior, do your own scholarship search. There's a scholarship search app called Scholly Search®, created by a young black man named Christopher Gray. Students use the app to find free full and partial college scholarships.

Use of the app is now free. Scholarships aren't just based on grades. There are some scholarships for high school students, college students, African Americans and other categories.

Also, The United Negro College Fund® has been around for decades. They still award college scholarships and grants to black students, doing well in school.

The scholarship search app creator was also going after his dream. In 2015, Christopher presented his idea to investors on Shark Tank.

Shark Tank is a TV program where millionaires invest their own money, time, marketing, and knowledge in businesses created by people chasing their dreams. Two of those millionaires invested in his idea and bought a percentage of his company.

In 2023, Christopher and his investors sold the company to Sallie Mae®, one of the largest college loan lenders. You may want to check out this app and the TV program. Christopher's story is another great example of the power of dreaming and not giving up on dreams.

Also, if you're old enough to work, try to find a job where the company offers their employees education benefits. Some companies offer a percentage of money to students for college, through scholarships or tuition discounts.
Chick-Fil-A restaurants offer "Remarkable Futures Scholarships" to their employees who are in high school and want to apply.
Chick-fil-a.com/remarkable-futures-scholarships. Check it out for complete, updated details.

They also offer high school students who are not employees to apply for another type of college scholarship. You can find out more information about it when you look up the Remarkable Futures one. Go ahead. Go after your dream and have some fun too. Going after your dream is work, but it's fun too! Enjoy the ride!

There are also college grants that you could apply for. Those grants pay all or some college tuition, based on your families' income. There's also other financial aid available.

If you graduated more than a few years ago, student loans could be your option for paying for college. Student loans have a very low rate and are payable, monthly, once you graduate from college. While working, start saving some money to put toward your loan. That way, you won't have as much debt upon graduating.

To cut down on cost, consider going first to a community college for 2 years. The tuition is cheaper. After the 2 years, you could transfer credits earned to a university to complete a 4-year degree. Find out in advance which/how many credits you'll be able to transfer. If that's not in your plan, you'll still have an Associate degree after the 2 years and could start a career from there.

If you'd prefer getting a certificate, going to a vocational/technical school/college would be a good option. Most certificate programs take less than 6 months or up to a year to complete. Some hands-on training to consider would be barber, plumber, personal trainer, roofer, mechanic, carpenter, graphic designer, chef, welder and jobs in the hotel/restaurant industry.

If you don't have a GED, getting one could be your first dream. Prepare to take the GED test. Maybe you dropped out of school because you were distracted, had trouble reading, family issues, or was simply bored. Whatever the reason was back then, right now, you have a second chance. Here are ways to get back what was missed.

It would be helpful to start your dream of getting a GED by preparing 90 days before taking the test. You could start by focusing on math and reading first. There are many math websites to choose from, for all grade levels.

Mathisfun.com would be a good one to start with. Math problems and step by step learning are provided. Choose the grade level most comfortable to you. After getting familiar with it, move to a higher grade level. Practicing math just 15 minutes a day for a week would help with getting back in the swing of things. The next week, move up to 30 minutes. You'll start solving problems faster and gain more confidence.

Starting off the same way with reading would be helpful too. Maybe the goal could be to start with 15 minutes and keep moving up until an hour is reached. You'll begin to read faster and gain more confidence. Read about things you're interested in or like. When you do, time will fly. If you're really into sports, maybe you could start reading about your favorite player and keeping up with how well he's playing.

When you come across unfamiliar words, look them up. In seconds, you could use your phone or a computer to find out their meaning. Just plug in your headset for privacy. No one knows every meaning. All of us have done and still do what's being suggested here, so you're not the only one.

Looking up words will help build vocabulary and confidence, while preparing for the GED test. It will also help with daily living. You could do the same thing when you come across words hard to pronounce.

Find and keep a quiet reading spot, it'll help you read with confidence and learn faster. Maybe reading in your room, bathroom, or a park, could help with privacy.

Or, you could even go to the library and use a study room. They're free.

When you get your GED, congratulations! But, don't stop there. Keep reading and practicing math. Keep learning new words and making sentences with them. Make it a habit. Keep getting better. Keep learning. The more you know the higher you can go.

These are just a few suggestions and examples for dreams. There are plenty more options available.

If you're still trying to figure out your dream, ask yourself questions listed on the next page. They'll lead you to the dream that's best for you. They'll help with starting a dream and making a plan.

Dream Planner

What do you already know how to do and get excited about?

What do you really enjoy and find yourself doing or wanting to do all the time?

What are your favorite things to do?

What do you admire?

What gets and keeps your attention?

What is it that you can't seem to get away from?

Write down what you want to do in life. Here are a few ways to get you started.

This is the thing I do.

_____

_____

These are the things I can do.

_____

_____

This is what I'm good at.

_____

_____

These are the things I'm best at.

_____

_____

Let me be clear. You're not chasing money. You're chasing your dream. Go after your dream, that thing that you love to do more than anything else. In time, the money will come with it. It will come in steps. At first, you'll start with a little. And it may stay that way for a while.

Be thankful for the little and have fun going after your dream. Be grateful for what you'll be accomplishing. If you don't appreciate the small, you will miss seeing progress. You won't enjoy the ride. You'll easily give up and quit. Being thankful will also help with keeping discouragement away, when movement is slow. If you write down progress as it's being made, looking at what was accomplished will lift you up.

If you go after something only because it pays a lot of money, you won't have the money. The money will have you. You'll always be thinking about money and getting more of it. That will make it easier to give in to the temptation of doing anything to get more of it.

Money can bring stuff into lives, but it can't bring happiness and peace of mind. Don't chase after money. Chase after your dream.

If you pick a dream from something you love to do, it won't feel like work. You'll be getting paid to do something you really enjoy. Every day won't be perfect. There will be headaches here and there, but you'll still be doing what you like and are good at.

If your dream is to eventually start your own business, still take care of your daily responsibilities.

Don't leave your regular job and go running after your dream. At the start of your dream, there won't always be enough steady money coming in. So, you'll have to keep your regular paying job. For a while, getting your dream started will be your extra job, your side hustle. Extra money will come from it. Save that money and keep building up your business.

Let me be clear. Everything mentioned here will take time, commitment, and hard work. But, it's doable and worth it. If you keep at it, you'll see progress and change.

And dads, important people, like your kids, will see it too. Children like to show off about their parents, especially little boys. They like to brag about their dads, what they're good at. When they're outside playing in the streets with other kids you can hear them saying my daddy did this.... My daddy can do that.... What they're really saying is, they want to be like their dads. They're proud of them. They're really saying my daddy did it. I can do it too.

When you start your dream and go after it, you'll be showing your kids how to dream and have goals. They'll be receiving direction and confidence.

You'll be showing them how they can have a good, positive life when they grow up. It'll stay with them while they're growing up and when they become men and women. You'll be proud of them. They'll pass it on to their sons and daughters. It'll keep on going.

There's no doubt that the little kids who competed in the cooking competitions had parents telling them they could be chefs or anything they wanted.

They started teaching and encouraging them to dream at a very early age. It gave them direction and confidence to become something in life.

To get your dream, you'll have to set goals. These are steps you prepare to push your dream forward. An important key to success is preparation. If you don't know where you're going, you can't get there. If you don't know how to get there, you won't get there.

If you go after your dream without first preparing, you will get discouraged when it's not moving at all or fast enough. If you prepare, by making a plan and sticking with it, you can win. That's where goal setting comes in. These are things that you will do every day to get to your dream. When done steadily, you'll reach your dream over time.

The key is to be specific. Example. What if you dream of becoming a chef? You'd have to be specific and say something like, *I want to be a chef in 2 years*. If you simply say *I want to be a chef someday*, it'll take a life time to get there. You'll only go after that dream every now and then, whenever you feel like it.

After being specific, find out which activities will help to reach that goal. Commit to doing those activities. Do something every day. Example. If you want to be a chef, some things you could write down to do would be:
I will practice cooking for a minimum of one hour each day;
I will read books and magazines to find out about different spices and flavors;
I will watch cooking shows to learn about different foods and get new ideas.

Think about what you can do long-term to reach that chef goal too. You could do things like: work in restaurant kitchens; learn on the job; take some cooking classes; get in a certificate program or go to college.

If your goal is to get a GED, say when you want to receive one. You could say, *I want to get my GED by the end of this year.* I will do something every day.

Some things you could write down to do would be:
I will take classes to prepare for the test;
I will get tutoring outside of class;
I will read at least 30 minutes each day;
(Ten-minute readings could be done 3 times during the day to reach the 30 minute goal)
I will practice and study basic math and word problems an hour a day;
If free in-person classes aren't available, I will get free online GED sample tests and practice;
I will get free on-line English grammar and math worksheets and practice.

Long term goals could be like:
I will learn meanings of new words every day;
(Each word has several meanings)
I will keep learning new ways to use math.

If you want to work in any of the areas listed at the beginning of this chapter, some things you can do every day would be:
I will practice what I already know;
I will practice at least an hour a day;
I will read books to find out more information.

Long term goals could be like: getting a job that uses that skill; learning more; taking a class; or going to college.

If you miss the goal "complete by" date don't shrug it off. Discover the reason and do something about it. Ask yourself questions. Did I miss doing something every day? Did I forget about my goal? Did I focus on something else important? Did I give up? If so, why? Did I think it was too hard? Did I change my mind about it?

Keep the right mindset with goal setting. If you see it as missing out on fun or other things, you won't stick with it. If you see the work and time put in as preparing you to buy a car, rent a house, buy a house, or get a better life, you'll stick with it.

One more thing about goals, setting them too high will frustrate you and you'll give up. Set realistic starter goals first. Smaller goals take shorter time, sometimes months or just under a year. Larger goals take longer.

Take little steps first. As you see results and get comfortable, set medium sized goals. After you reach those, you'll automatically know what to do and how to get to where you want to be. Slow and steady wins the race, slow and steady.

Pay attention to what works and what doesn't. Learn as you go. Don't use the excuse *I've tried it and it didn't work out*. Do what's going to help move you closer to your dream and a better life.

Being disciplined isn't easy, but it's worth it. It won't be easy all the time. If you do the hard things now, later on you will see how much it was worth it.

What am I really saying? Find your dream. Plan and work your goal. Go after it, until you get there. Success is up to you.

A better life is up to you. You get to decide, no one else. Just you. Do a good job. Do your very best. Where you come from or how you look doesn't determine how far you can go in life. You determine that. It'll take small changes. One at a time.

IMPORTANT INFORMATION TO KNOW

- **GOAL OR OBJECTIVE**
  A goal or objective is a want that a person has to reach results for something specific. Steps for results are planned out, done over time, and regularly followed. Goals can be short or long term.

- **SHORT TERM GOAL**
  A short-term goal is something you want to get or do soon. It's something that can be done within a day, week, month, 3 months, 6 months, or up to a year.

- **LONG TERM GOAL**
  A long-term goal is something you want to get or do in the future. It's something that will take more time to get results. It'll take longer than a year or several years to reach.

- **DISCIPLINE**
  Discipline is when a person decides to take action to complete a job or duty regardless of circumstances. He consistently chooses to reach planned goal when delays, obstacles, circumstances, or lack of motivation or energy are present.

- **SUCCESSFUL GOAL**
  Successful goal is reached when a person gets and stays prepared to reach a goal. Once new opportunities present themselves the person quickly takes action.

CHAPTER FOUR

Hands On Your Dream

If you don't know how to deal with unexpected things when going for your dream, discouragement will easily come. It will cause the smallest things to frustrate you and keep from getting to the end.

Maybe that has already happened. If it has, here's a chance to start over and make it work. This chapter will help with staying on track. It'll help to keep going and stay in hope.

It'll show what to expect when dreaming and goal setting begin. Delays, setbacks and interruptions won't be a problem. You'll know how to handle them and make adjustments. You will be prepared and can easily bounce back and stay on track. Now, let's go get that dream!

Stay ready. Plan ahead. When plans are already in place before the unexpected happens, chances of success are higher. Doubt and stress won't be able to show up. Confidence will be there. You'll know you're going somewhere. Ahead of time, think about two or three solutions to use if something unexpectedly interrupts your dream. It'll help with staying on track.

Interruptions big and small will have to be dealt with. Being unmotivated will be one of those small interruptions. Some days you will wake up in the morning and won't feel like doing anything toward your dream. You will have to shake off that feeling and get going. A plan has to already be in place to talk yourself into doing something to move.

A solution has to already be there to help with staying on that positive path to better. If words or thoughts start coming about not feeling like doing anything, it's going to zap all of your energy. That energy will be needed to go after that dream or goal. Once moving forward begins, you will see that you can do amazing things.

If something bigger happens, like family or work issues, take care of those things, but have two or three solutions already in place to keep going. If you stay away from your dream too long, it'll be easy to forget about it and not make progress. Commitment, focus, and determination will have to be and stay there. Belief in that dream will have to be there too. Belief in making a difference has to stay there. If these things aren't there, that dream will never get off the ground.

Here's something else that will help with that. Try writing down why a certain dream was chosen. Doing so will help to stay encouraged and keep hope. If you get off track, look at why that dream was chosen and why the decision was made to go for it!

Each day, motivate and encourage yourself. That's one of the reasons you were encouraged to start saying good things about yourself. Saying those things will help when the unexpected happens. Doing so will have to become a habit. Don't let all the hard work or fear of not being able to do better put a stop to doing better. Don't let hard work and time go to waste. Press on. You can do it. You have what it takes to win in life. Make the decision to keep moving.

Keep doing it. It's natural for us to think some things are hard when it's our first time doing them. When we have to do them the next time, they're a little easier. After the second time, we don't have to make ourselves do them or put in the effort. We do them without even thinking.

Guide negative thoughts to the positive when delays come. Think of what can be done instead of what can't. Stick with the plan. Keep looking to where you want to be. You must keep yourself motivated and inspired. Keep talking about the way you want to be. All through the day, get in the habit of saying good things about you and your future. Keep going. You will get closer. Thoughts may tell you it's never going to work out. That's not how your story ends. Stay focused on your brighter future.

Picture being in that dream. Be so determined that you could almost reach out your hand and feel it. Keep a picture of that dream in sight. See yourself doing what you ultimately want to do. Picture becoming what you ultimately want to be. See yourself working hard, doing what needs to be done to get there.

Keep a daily reminder. Draw or take a picture of how you imagine life will be when that dream is reached. Put the picture in a place where it can be seen every day. Keep a picture of it in your head too. Imagine what it would be like getting there. Think about how satisfied and happy you'll be after getting there.

- **See yourself filling out new employee paperwork to start your new job.**
- **See yourself taking the written driver's license test and passing.**

- See yourself unpacking boxes in the house you saved up money for so long to buy.
- See yourself starting over, making good choices, and living a better life.
- See yourself studying for the GED, confidently taking the test, and passing with a high score.
- See yourself walking onto a college campus to start classes.

See yourself there! Stay focused and work the plan you set in the previous chapter. It'll help to keep a positive mood, instead of one that's constantly flip/flopping. The desire to keep switching between being excited and not wanting to do anything will be removed.

Keep the right focus. If focus stays on what's not working or how long it's taking, you'll lose sight of your dream. It'll be easier to forget about progress already made. A habit of starting/stopping, starting/stopping will come. That dream or goal won't be seen as important anymore.

When you zoom in on time the farther away your dream will look than it actually is. If worry and how long it's taking are there, progress won't be seen. That's why it's so important to say good things about you and do something every day. Keep moving forward and seeing the end.

- See yourself in your own business, flicking on lights and flipping a sign over to open.
- See yourself filling out applications by yourself and getting a job.
- See yourself smiling and driving a car that you worked so hard to buy.

- See yourself putting a key in the door to an apartment, one that you picked out and put a deposit on.
- See yourself smiling because you accomplished something good that you or other people never thought would or could happen.

Results can be seen when daily commitment is there. If consistent, small steps are taken, you will clearly see huge footprints of progress. When movement is constant and daily, the end will be in sight. When your eyes are kept on the goal, you will end up where you're aiming at.

To win you must have the right mind set. You have to keep thinking positively, be courageous, and determined. Delays and situations will come, but you have to keep at it.

Do you remember times when you sat around with friends watching a big football or basketball game and your team wasn't playing well? All through the game, your team was struggling. Players were getting knocked down a lot and pushed back by their opponents.

It looked like they were losing. They couldn't get enough points to get ahead. There wasn't an option to quit in the middle of the game. They had to keep playing until the game was over. They had to keep going. To finish, they had to pull up mental toughness, keep playing, and telling themselves they could win. Each player had to focus on what needed to be done to win, instead of focusing on what the other team was doing. When they kept that focus, they either improved and got close to winning or ended up winning the game.

You have to really want it. If you choose to focus, you're always still in the game. Stay in the game. Tackle the setbacks. Break through the negative words. Push through the tough times. You're stronger than your circumstances. Keep a target on winning. If delays come, it won't be over. Just quickly get back on track. Keep moving forward.

To break through tough times, positive words have to be continually said. I can do it. I will do this. I will become what I've been working hard to be. I've come too far to stop now. I've made up my mind and I'm not turning back. High expectations have to stay there. Expectations give hope. You have to have courage and care deeply about the results. Keep hope alive. Keep remembering how much progress was already gained.

Focus on the end. Don't quit. If quitting comes in, it will become a normal thing. You'll never see how high you can really go. If thoughts are always on how hard something is, you'll be pulled in the direction of quitting.

To win, more important things like good choices will be needed. Making right decisions will determine if there's a better future. If you're committed to reaching dreams and goals your daily choices will have to be guided by that commitment. That means the decision to say no to some things must be made.

Saying no to drugs, alcohol, and violence will have to be some of those choices. Drugs and alcohol hijack your freedom and holds your future hostage. Violence hijacks your freedom and holds your future hostage. They mess up your mind, body, and life. Those things only provide temporary relief and return with more permanent destruction.

They tear down and destroy you, your family, and other people's families.

If you're already having issues with drugs and alcohol, I encourage you to seek help. Choose to make good decisions. Do something that you will be proud of. Be fair to yourself. Give yourself a chance.

It's important to think about tomorrow, next week, next month, every time you make a decision. Say no to things and choices holding you back. Say no to drugs, alcohol, and violence. Stay free. Walk away. Keep walking and head toward a good dream and a better life.

Choice of time spent will also be important. Is what time being spent on building you up or tearing you down and taking away hope? If what time is spent on isn't making you better, something to be proud of, it's not needed.

You must keep choosing to do the right things. Choosing right is freeing. Think of your choices like spending money. Once you take it out of your pocket and buy something, it's gone. Choose wisely.

You write the ending to your story. You do that by the decisions you make. Do those things that bring out the best in you. Hang around people who bring out the best in you. In the end, it'll be worth it.

Decide to say no to people telling you to take the fast way out. Taking the fast way out, by doing wrong and illegal things, only creates more problems. Those decisions steal your freedom and make life much harder than it needs to be. It's a long, expensive price to pay.

There's no hope or peace in that. You end up doing things that hurt yourself and other people. You end up spending every day paying for it, watching your back, always looking over your shoulder.

Instead of choosing that life, remember that you're better than that. You can learn anything. You can do anything. Be fair to you. Give yourself a chance.
Look forward to the dream that's coming your way. When you stay persistent, you're always close to it. Stay focused. Stay expectant.

Work hard and give it time. Positive rewards will be the result. Your family, friends, and people around you will see it too. Some may even end up saying, *if that happened for him, maybe it could happen for me too.*

GOOD HABITS FOR WINNING

- Stay in the Habit of Saying Good Things About You

- Get in the Habit of Staying Motivated

- Get in the Habit of Reading and Learning

- Get in the Habit of Doing Your Very Best

- Stay in the Habit of Keeping Your Cool

- Get in the Habit of Controlling Your Actions and Reactions

- Stay in the Habit of Being Disciplined

CHAPTER FIVE

Money Matters

This chapter includes information to help with a first job, a job change, and everyday money tips. You'll learn what to expect while searching for a job and after getting one.

Once your job search begins and after being hired, this information will be needed. A complete list of these categories follows these pages. This section provides additional information for some of them.

IMPORTANT JOB INFORMATION TO KNOW

When applying for jobs, a resume' will be needed. A resume' is a single sheet of neatly typed information that lists your work experience, education, and skills. Dates of recent experience are listed first. Depending on the type of job applying for, a cover letter may also be needed.

A cover letter is a three to four paragraphs letter included with some job applications. This letter is used to show interest in a position, why you're applying at that particular company, and your top qualifications. The first paragraph is the introductory paragraph. Applicants briefly state who they are, the job applying for, and interest in the job.

The rest of the letter states what motivated the person to apply for that particular job. Applicants explain how they can meet the companies needs by sharing how their skills and job experiences have prepared them for the open position. Applicants show what makes them the best person for the job. The end of the letter includes how, and the best way, to be contacted.

Every job doesn't require a cover letter. The letter has the current date, your name, and contact information. It's addressed to the hiring manager of the company and includes the companies' name and full address.

If you have a computer, blank resume' and cover letter samples are already included on it. Just go to Word and click on new document, and they'll pop up. If you don't have a computer, use a cellphone to look up sample cover letters or type in Microsoft Word cover letters, to see samples. There is also help available at some places mentioned in this book.

A computer will be needed to type the letter and fill-out applications. If you don't own one, most public libraries have computers available for free use. No library card is needed.

After the resume' and cover letter are complete, read them and check for correct spelling and grammar. Have someone who already has a job re-check them for you. Once saved on the computer or a flash drive, you're ready to apply. It may also be a good idea to print out extra resume' copies for interviews, just in case. Make sure copies are neat, clean, and unfolded.

If you're a high school student and applying for your first job and don't have experience, apply anyway. Under job title write down student. In the work experience section list "other experience". Begin to list some things that could be used to apply for that job.

Example. If you're or were on a sports team or school club, you have experience that is needed for all jobs/businesses.

You help the team win by knowing how to:

- Work as a team to get the job done
- Manage time (you know the importance of being on time and how being late affects the entire team/business)
- Listen well and follow instructions (follow coaches/leader's instructions)
- Be flexible (easily make adjustments when plans have to change, switching plays/helping out in another position or role)
- Think quickly

If you're a captain on the team, also add leadership skills. You're experienced in giving and receiving instructions. You're good at making decisions and explaining yourself. All of these things are important for any job. If information like this is included, your application should stand out. It will show hiring managers you're serious about working.

When looking for a job, help from other people will be needed. They will be needed for references. All companies ask for at least three references. They usually ask for 2 professional references and 1 personal reference. Some may simply ask for 3 references, leaving the choice up to the applicant.

A professional reference is a statement given by one of your former supervisors. It's an email, written letter, or phone conversation telling what your duties were while at that company and if you'd be a good candidate for the position you're applying for.

A personal reference is a statement telling what type of person you are. It's given by someone you know, such as a friend, teacher, coach, or counselor. When choosing personal references, make sure to choose people who will say good things about you and your ability to do the job. Also, ask them ahead of time if their names, numbers, and emails could be used for references. That way, when they're contacted, they'll make time to respond. Bring the list of references when filling out applications. You may also want to bring a printed, unfolded copy to interviews.

Most companies offer employees company benefits. When applying, make sure to see what type of benefits they offer. If no information is included in the ad, ask about them at the end of the interview, if they aren't brought up. Benefit information is included later in this chapter.

For a Successful Job Search

When applying for a job, skipping over a job because you don't meet all the qualifications isn't necessary. Even if you don't meet all the requirements, still apply. It can't hurt to try. Who knows? Maybe you're the right person for another position at that company.

Take a little extra time to go over duties for the job you're applying for. You'll know which things are most important to the company. See how many of those things were part of your duties on past jobs. Include them in your cover letter and talk about them most during the interview.

While looking for a permanent job, consider temporary jobs too. If you've already completed high school or want a change in job type, this could be another option.

Temporary agencies provide temporary jobs that sometime turn into permanent ones. Many construction jobs are found through temporary agencies. Working with one is also a good way to make money while looking for a permanent job. Work experience and new skills would also be gained.

If you happen to go to job fairs to apply for jobs, here's a tip. Dress like you're going on an interview. Most times, those companies aren't just taking applications. They're interviewing and hiring on the spot.

Common Interview Questions

These are just a few common questions interviewers ask. They may ask some or all of them. Just expect to be asked more or similar questions like these. Take time to get familiar with them. The more comfortable you are the more likely you'll do well. If you'd like more examples, ask someone who has been working a while to provide some or check job search websites.

1. Why do you want to work here?
Please don't answer this question by saying you need the money or just need a job. The interview won't go well with those answers. Besides, the person already knows you need the money and a job. The company doesn't want to know how they can help you. They want to know how you can help them.

You're expected to answer that question by sharing the good things you already know about the company, what you like about it, and why you chose to apply there.
Then tell how your skills and experience could help fit in with the company.

2. What are your strengths?

This question is being asked to show what you're good at and how those skills can help in the open position. The hiring manager also wants to know how you handle difficulties on the job.

Example. Maybe you're good at being flexible (you can change work styles quickly). You don't mind change. Maybe you're focused (you keep doing a job until it's finished). Maybe you're dedicated (you care about companies you've worked for and looked out for them). Maybe you know importance of teamwork (you work well with co-workers to get the job done). Whatever your strengths are, be prepared to give good examples of when those strengths were used on a job.

High school students, see student examples for this question on the previous page.

3. What are your weaknesses?

This question is being asked to show what you need improvements in or training. It's also asked to see if you're able to receive helpful criticism from a supervisor and can make changes to get better.

Example. If you don't have much computer experience, admit that. But emphasize the positive. Include what you're doing to improve in that area and gain experience.

Maybe a supervisor gave you a helpful criticism for a way to do your job a little faster. You made changes by being more aware of time, moving faster and getting better. For any answer about helpful criticism, make sure to stress that you're open to receiving feedback. And when you are given helpful criticism by a supervisor, don't take it personally. Be open to receiving it. It'll help with learning more and being better.

4. Why should I hire you?

This question is asked to see if you'd be a good fit for the position. A good way to answer this question would be by convincing the person you're the best person for the job. Tell what you can do, what you have done, and how you can help the company.

5. What are some ways people would describe you?

This is a similar question to what are your strengths? Share good qualities about yourself that could help you succeed in the open position.

Example. Maybe people describe you as hardworking, punctual (you're always on time), detailed (you take time to do a job right, in an organized way). You're a problem solver. All of these qualities could be used in any position. Be prepared to give examples when those qualities were used in past positions or professional situations.

6. Where or how do you see yourself in 5 years?

This question is asked to see how well the job fits with your general career goals. The hiring manager wants to know if your expectations fit the open position, if you're interested in the job, and will still be interested over time.

Example. If you're interviewing for a food industry position and want to be a sales person in five years, you most likely won't be seen as a good fit. But, if you're interviewing for a food industry position and want to be a restaurant supervisor or manager in 5 years, your expectations would fit in with current and long-term positions.

In addition to these questions, hiring managers may also make this statement. Tell me about yourself. The person isn't asking about your personal life, home life, or where you're from. He wants you to briefly share more details about important work experience, skills, and your good qualities. He wants to know how those things will line up with skills required for the job.

Remember to have a good attitude when applying for the job and interviewing. Keep that same positive attitude after you get it. You will need that positivity to do a good job.

Day Before Interview

Know the kind of business or company applying to

Know how you can benefit the company by working there

Know why you want to work for the company

Practice answering interview questions with someone who already has a job. If the interview is scheduled more than a day ahead, practice every day. The more you practice the more confident and comfortable you'll be. Make it a habit to practice interviewing while looking for jobs. If no one is available to help with practicing, practice saying the questions and answers out loud.

Day of Interview

Dress appropriately, when going on interviews. Put your best forward. Take time to get clothes ready the day before the interview. Make sure clothes are wrinkle free, clean, and neat. For some of you, wearing oversized baggy pants, that slide down as you walk, may be "the style". If those are the only pants you have to wear, make the look work for the interview. Make sure a belt is worn that stops them from falling.

Companies want employees to dress the way that they ask. Some may even ask employees to wear uniforms. If you start off in the food industry, preparing food, you may be asked to wear a hair covering. No one wants to get ready to bite into a piece of food and see hair in it.

Employers aren't trying to tell you how to dress. It' not personal. They're simply telling you how they want employees to represent their business. Nothing's wrong with that.

While interviewing, **make good eye contact** with the hiring manager. Doing so will help with paying attention and showing interest. It'll also let the person know that you have answers, and are not avoiding them.

Go alone to interviews. Bringing friends or kids will be distracting during the interview. Having to stop children from crying, running around, or talking will take away your concentration and that of the hiring manager.

Having your cell phone ringing or receiving texts during interviews will be distracting too. Focus will be needed for what is being asked. **Turning off the cell phone** a few minutes before the interview will help with that. It'll also show respect for the person doing the hiring.

Tips for a Good Job Experience

Call your supervisor to let him or her know when you're running late. When the supervisor is called, it gives the person enough time to make changes until you get there. **Show up when scheduled for work**. Being tired or not feeling like going to work isn't a good reason to skip work. You have to get up and get going.

Missing work because it's your birthday or another special occasion wouldn't be a good choice either. Celebrate after work. If a day off for your birthday or special occasion is wanted, set-up the day with a supervisor weeks ahead. When supervisors are asked in advance, the work schedules can be adjusted. Also, if company benefits are offered, that day could be used as a paid vacation day, instead of an unpaid day. Show up. People on the job are counting on you. Show up for you too.

Always do a good job. Cutting corners or doing sloppy work isn't the way to go. Short cuts create problems. The same job ends up being done twice, because it wasn't done right. Learn how the finished job is supposed to look, when it's done right. Use it as a guide. A good job is one in which you can stand back, fold your arms, and look at the finished work. With a smile or a happy dance, you can say, *wow! That looks good. It's done right. I did that!* You will feel good about yourself and the accomplishment. Customers will be happy too.

Be a person of integrity. Do a good job when the boss is around and when he is not. When we do a good job no matter who is around it shows we care about doing good work. We're doing a good job for ourselves. We're honest and do good work. It shows the company and customers that quality is important to us. No one is being cheated out of good results.

Don't be afraid to ask questions. If instructions are unclear, ask the person to explain again. Supervisors expect employees to ask questions, especially new ones. Other people being trained may also have the same question, but are afraid to ask. Some people are afraid to ask questions when they hear something that they don't understand or know. To keep from looking foolish, they pretend they know what the other person is saying. The problem with doing that is, they never get what they need. The smart thing to do is to ask questions. Get what you need. Remember, they hired you because they believed in your ability to do the job. Keep that same belief and ask.

When being trained, **listen**. Pay attention so that you'll know how to do the job and can remember what to do. You'll be nervous the first time. That's okay. It's natural. Everyone is nervous on a new job. Don't let that take away the focus of listening. Pay attention. When the time comes to use what was taught, you'll remember.

Get along with co-workers. Be nice. Treat people how you want to be treated. People will want to work with you. You will have a better experience working with them too. Be aware of your tone of voice. People respond in a good way when the right tone is used. After all, the goal is to have everyone working together to get the job done. Right?

All jobs have a certain number of problems. But, they also have good times. Try hard to get along with others. Some new friendships may even be made.

REASONS PEOPLE MAY LOSE JOBS

Not being on time for work can cause problems. Why? Every job is important. Each one is connected to the other. They're all needed to make a business run smoothly. Get and stay in the habit of being on time. It shows respect for co-workers and the company.

If you struggle with managing time, practice getting better at it before starting a job. One way to help with that is to see how much can be done within a certain amount of time.

Try this. Set your phone, watch, or clock for 10 or 15 minutes. See how many things can be done to get ready for work, before the alarm goes off. After it does, set it again. Do some more things.

Here's something else to try. Turn on your favorite song and start getting ready. When the song ends, stop. Notice how many and what things were done during that time. Put on another song, and do the same thing. Most songs last up to 4 minutes or a little longer. You'll be surprised at what can be done within that amount of time. You'll have to make sure you don't get caught up in the beat. It would be easy to start singing and dancing and end up forgetting about getting ready.

Getting in the habit of doing any one of these things will help manage time. You'll have an idea of the total amount of time needed to get out the door.

Not having **a good attitude** day in and day out can affect the mood of everyone at work. Our attitude is an outward expression of our inward feelings. Our attitude speaks louder than our words. People see our attitude without us saying a word. If we're stressed out or upset about something that happened before work, we can't take it out on other people.

We have to get ourselves together so that we'll have a good day and co-workers and customers will too. Our attitude draws people to us or chases them away. Have a good attitude and keep people coming.

Cellphone use or texting while working isn't usually allowed. Companies ask employees to use these when on assigned breaks or during lunch. Talking on the phone or texting while working isn't professional. Customers aren't given full attention. And you're likely to make some mistakes that normally wouldn't be made. Remember times at the grocery store checking out and the cashier was on the phone or texting? Didn't that make you wonder if he or she was really paying attention to ringing up your stuff?

Not following company rules can be a major problem. Rules are there to make sure business runs smoothly, that everyone is safe, and employees are treated fairly. Following rules is part of being on the team. If you have issues with being told what to do, you'll have to work on fixing that. Without company rules or life rules, everything would be a crazy mess.

What if players on both football teams did whatever they wanted, whenever they wanted, during games? Helmets and shoulder pads would be crashing everywhere. Sounds of knees popping and arms cracking would be heard the entire time. No one would win. No one could win.

And what about driving? Suppose drivers didn't stop at red lights because they didn't feel like it. Cars would be smashing into each other like bumper cars. Drivers, passengers, and people walking would be hurt and killed. Respect rules. Follow rules on the job. Follow rules in life.

GETTING TO SUPERVISOR LEVEL

If the goal is to move up, pay attention to the supervisors. Learn from them. Take notice of how they handle problems, treat customers, and co-workers. Watch how they do their jobs.

Also, check with your manager for continuing education training like one-day workshops, seminars, or classes. Many companies provide or approve free advanced training programs.

As time goes on, you will get better on the job. Confidence will come. That'll be a good thing. If you keep doing well, promotion to supervisor could happen. If it does, great job! In the process, don't become full of yourself. Stay humble. Learn some more. Keep doing a good job. More good things will come your way.

Keep working hard and treating people right. If co-workers are really busy and struggling to keep up with customers, help them. Treat people how you'd like to be treated. You'll need co-workers. Everyone on the team will be needed.

You'll be the quarterback of the team. But, if you don't have people to block for you or have someone to throw the ball to, you won't be able to do the job. Everyone is important and needed. Work together. The job will get done better and faster.

If you're that kind of supervisor, people will want to be a part of your team. They'll want to work with and learn from you.

WINNING CUSTOMER SERVICE

On the job, expect the best, but know that every day won't be perfect. There will be times when some customers will be rude. There will be moments when some things won't go just right. During those times, keep smiling and doing a good job. Keep treating customers with respect. Avoid issues and stay helpful. If you slip and say something that you shouldn't, just apologize. Say sorry and move on.

Provide good customer service. Every time we go to a store, restaurant, or any place of business, we're the customers. We want to be treated well and with respect. When customers come on your job, they too want to be treated that way. Be nice. Be respectful. Be professional. That mainly means controlling your emotions. That means you're not cursing or calling people names. You're watching what you say to people and controlling tone and volume of your voice. You don't have to yell to be heard. Choose to control yourself, especially when a customer is upset.

Find out why the customer isn't happy. Listen to the person. When we're upset, we want to be heard. We don't want to be cut off when speaking and brushed aside. We want to explain what went wrong. When the other person is silent and really listens, we feel respected. Treat customers the same way. Avoid interrupting them. Let them speak and listen. **Try to solve the problem.** If you can't, let the customer know that the supervisor can help. Excuse yourself and go and get the supervisor. Even if you end up not being able to help the customer, at least you tried.

Sometimes, the issue isn't the customer, it's us. We all have situations outside of work. Not adjusting our mood before getting to work can affect our co-workers and customers. If we're going through something, we have to take a few minutes to get ourselves together, before going to work.

To avoid problems, we have to shake off the sour mood and leave it outside. If it's not left there, there's a good chance the wrong thing will be said or something is said the wrong way to co-workers and customers. Or, we will see everything as stressful. We'll treat customers like they're there to get on our nerves, bother us, or we're doing them a great favor.

Why is great customer service so important? Great customer service is very important because no business can survive without customers. A business can have great products, but if it doesn't value customers, the customers will easily spend their money someplace else. No one wants to give their money to a business and be treated poorly.

When a customer has a good experience at a restaurant, store, or any place of business, they may tell 2 or 3 people about that experience and company. When a customer has a very bad experience, they'll tell twice or three times as many people about that company. They'll tell anybody who will listen.

The company wants customers to have a good experience. They want them to keep coming back. They need them to keep coming back in order to pay employees. When customers enjoy themselves, they come back. When customers are happy, they return more often and keep spending. When they keep coming back, you have a job. You get paid. Doesn't that make sense?

If you do a good job, some customers may even come back looking for you, because you treated them so well.

One final thing, if you end up working somewhere that you don't want to stay, please leave the right way. When you do, you'll have a company that you could go back to.

Give a one or two week notice to your supervisor. Don't just walk out or tell someone off or post an angry "I quit" video on social media. You may have or want to go back to that company, to work in another department or the same one. If you leave the wrong way, you won't be able to do that. And what do you think will happen when you list that company as past work experience? And what if that video goes viral and managers at other places where you applied see it?

In addition to leaving the right way, always make sure you have another job to go to before leaving the current one.

Now, that we've covered paychecks, let's move on to other money tips. This section is not about sitting atop stacks of money, like some entertainers seen in videos. Even the people in those spots don't really live that way. Most of us don't have money to waste. Here you'll see real life money matters. Here are ways to help keep more money in your pocket. They will help with buying or doing a few fun things you'd like to do too.

Part of getting better will be through saving money. Most of us can't buy a car, house, or other important things, without first having enough money. That takes saving and discipline. If you get in the habit of saving now, it'll be easier when it's time to buy those things, later on.

Having that first job is exciting. On pay day, you want to buy and celebrate. Everybody wants to have some fun spending money, especially after working hard for it. While having fun spending, it would be a good idea to save some of it. Have you heard the saying, save for a rainy day? Well, that's what you'd be doing.

If something important comes up, there will be some money to help take care of it. You won't have to stress as much about it.

Maybe you could try to set aside $20.00, $15.00, or $10.00 from each pay check. Use that money as a start up to saving. You can do it. Think about it. That amount is probably spent on fast-food, snacks, and small things anyway, without you even thinking about it.

If those amounts are too high, start saving just $5.00. In a few months, start saving a higher amount. You might be thinking, how can $5.00 make a difference? It'll add up and help to get in the habit of saving. Put the saved money somewhere you can't easily get to it.

When the higher paying jobs come, you will know about saving and how to keep more money. If the habit of managing small amounts is there, you'll know how to manage larger amounts later. You won't easily blow it. Have you heard about people who win big lotteries and end up broke in one or two years? That's going backwards. The goal is to move ahead.

When saving, temptation to buy things not needed will come. When you're walking in a store or past a store window, stuff will be yelling buy me! Buy me! Spend! Don't listen. Be strong. Don't give in. Stick with the plan.

Over time, a difference and progress will be made. Saving would also help with paying bills on time. Doing so would help to create and build credit needed to rent an apartment or eventually buy a house.

If you've worked before and are changing jobs, these tips could help you too. Another way to keep more money is to take care of the things already owned. Doing so helps them last longer. Money won't have to be spent to keep replacing things. That money could be used for something important.

When enough money is saved for a car, take care of the car after getting it. Starting off with a used car may be a good choice. They're much cheaper. Take time to look for a good, affordable one. Before buying, make sure it's in good shape. Try to look for one that's less than 4 years old, has low mileage, and well kept. Maybe someone who knows about cars could check it out with you. A reliable car will be needed to get back and forth to work. Getting one that's falling apart, and has bad tires, will keep costing money and time.

After working a while, you may want to get the most expensive name brand phones, clothes, tennis shoes, and other things. Those people who own those brands are already crazy rich. No disrespect. Instead of making their names bigger, why not use that money for your name? Your name is just as important as theirs. Why not use that money to help you?

Why not use it as a start to put your name on a car that you can buy and drive? Why not use it as a start to put your name on a house that you can buy and live in?

Why not use it as a start to put your name on a bank account? Why not use it as a start to put your name on a business that you can start and pass on to your children or family?

Any one or all of these things could be yours, if you're willing to be consistent with saving and working hard. It won't come overnight, but if you keep moving towards your goal, it'll happen.

Another important thing to know about is prioritizing. That simply means knowing in which order to do things to reach a goal or get a job done. Example. If you want to manage time better for work or something important, figure out the best way to get ready.

Should you start with what is shorter or longer? It may seem better to do the shorter things first, since they take less time. In some cases, that'd be the way to go. However, some small things easily turn into bigger ones, using more time. If the longer things are done first, there won't be enough time to get the other things done. There's a third and best option. The goal should be to do the most important thing first. If something happens or comes up that would affect total time, the most important thing would already be done. It'd be easier to adjust to the change and still do the other things.

Suppose it takes a total of one hour to get ready for work. To find out the most important, think about everything needed to be done to get out the door on time. Include making and eating breakfast. If you were running late, which one thing could only be done from home? It can't be done in the car, on the bus, while walking, or when you get to work. And it can't go undone. When you answer that question, you'll be able to see what's most important. It's that thing you'll have to do first every time.

To figure out what should be 2nd. and so on, do the same thing you did to find the most important. Carry that same kind of thinking over to prioritizing bill payments and budgeting money.

We already know it's important to pay rent, lights, and phone. Suppose the rent is $900.00 and together the light and phone bills are $400.00? Which do you pay first? It may seem better to pay the lights first, because you need lights and it's cheaper. Having a phone is important too. However, without an apartment or house there won't be any lights. Calling the electric company and asking for more time to pay the bill would help with the lights. If you have to skip the phone payment for that month and put money toward rent, that would help. Landlords don't usually let you pay rent late. So, the most important thing would be to budget for rent first.

A budget is an easy way in which we plan how our money will be spent and saved each month. It gives us a picture of where we are right now and where we want to be in the future. **Managing your money tells the money where to go, instead of it pulling you in many, hopeless directions**. It helps you get ahead. It gives hope for a better future.

Without a budget, getting an apartment, car, or buying a house won't be possible. If you're serious about living a better life, this is something that has to be done.

Each month won't be perfect. Money may be tight. Other important things could come up. When they do, think about your goal. Then, stick to your budget as close as possible. You're budgeting with a purpose. You're saving for a reason. Saving is taking you somewhere. Be determined to get there.

A budget is started by writing down the total income for the month. Then add up all of your bills/expenses and savings for the month. Begin with the most important bills/expenses first, such as food, rent, and lights. Before the beginning of the month, subtract the total monthly bills/additional expenses from your total monthly income. A sample budget follows these pages.

When making your budget, plan and act like more money isn't coming in. It'll force you to use the amount of money that's already there. The chances of sticking with the budget will be high.

But, if a budget is made with thoughts of more money coming when you get paid in two weeks, spending won't stop. You will be constantly telling yourself you'll put the money back, but never will. You won't be able to put it back anyway, because that money will be used to create the budget for the entire month. You can do more with less, when you don't have an option. If that's all you have, you'll make it last and work.

What if you ride a bus to work and never seem to have enough bus fare? That problem could be solved by managing your money with a budget. Before spending money from your check, figure out the cost for riding the bus for a month. Take out that amount from your check first. It'll remove the trouble of trying to get to work without bus fare and take away stress.

Maybe you'd like to buy a car? Saving and budgeting would help with getting there. Look for ways to cut back on other expenses, like a phone, tennis shoes, and small things. Get a cheaper phone plan. Buy less expensive tennis shoes. Cut back on barbershop visits. Stop buying little things here and there. Those things add up. Save the money and put it towards a car purchase.

Suppose you buy a $7.00 lunch every day that you work? If you bring your lunch from home for 4 days and only buy lunch on Fridays, you'd save $112.00 a month. At the end of the year, that would total $1232.00. That's money toward a down payment on a car. It would be a great start! When that amount is reached, keep saving. The more money you use as a down payment the lower your monthly car payments will be. It'll be easier to make payments each month. During a year, you'll be getting a tax refund. Use a large chunk or all of it to add to your down payment or start saving for insurance.

If you find other ways to cut back, you'd save even more. You'd be able to plan and clearly see when there would be enough to buy a car. Making small sacrifices like these and sticking to them will help with buying a car. Taking a bus year after year will be over. Always do the most important thing first.

One more thing, don't try to cut back on everything all at once, you'll get stressed about saving. It'll be seen as too much and frustration will come. That's why bringing lunch for 4 days instead of 5 was recommended. Buying lunch on just Fridays leaves a way to relax and not think about saving. It'll increase chances of sticking with your goal.

Sample Basic Monthly Budget
for 2 Working Adults

TOTAL MONTHLY INCOME $2170.00

Most important monthly bills/expenses

Food $400

Rent $900

Lights $200

Phone $120

Save (8%) $173.60

$2170.00 x 8% (0.08) = $173.60

Total for most important monthly bills/expenses $1793.60

$2170.00 (total monthly income) minus

$1793.60 (total most important) = $376.40

TOTAL REMAINING MONTHLY INCOME $376.40

ADDITIONAL MONTHLY EXPENSES

Bus fare – $90.00 x 2 (2 people) = $180.00

$2.25 (one-way daily bus fare)

$4.50 (round-trip daily bus fare)

Based on a five-day work week

$4.50 x 5 days = $22.50 per week

$22.50 x 4 weeks = $90.00 a month

$ 90.00 per month - per person

Total for monthly bus fare - $180.00

Personal hygiene

Soap – $15.00/10 pack bars

Toothpaste - $7.50 (6 tubes at 1.25 each)

Deodorant – $5.00 (4 sticks at 1.25 each

Other - $30.00

Total for monthly personal hygiene – $57.50

Sample Basic Monthly Budget
for 2 Working Adults

ADDITIONAL MONTHLY EXPENSES CONTINUED

Cleaning

Detergent – $7.50 (cleans 25 loads)

Washing machine use costs $27.00

($2.25 per load

Based on 3 loads per week

$2.25 x 3 loads = $6.75

$6.75 x 4 weeks = $27.00)

$27.00 per month

Dryer use costs $24.00

$2.00 per 1-hour dry time

Based on one hour x 3 loads = $6.00

$6.00 x 4 weeks = $24.00

$24.00 per month

Dish liquid - $4.00

Bleach/cleaner – $5.00

Total for monthly cleaning $67.50

TOTAL FOR ALL ADDITIONAL EXPENSES - $305.00

(Bus fare $180.00, Personal hygiene, $57.50, Monthly cleaning $67.50)

Total remaining monthly income ($376.40 minus Total all additional monthly expenses $305.00 = $71.40)

Total money remaining - $71.40

Total remaining is used for something fun or whatever you want. Note: If you know you have the same amount each month for fun things to do, you won't feel the need to overspend. It'll be easier to stick with the budget.

If the costs for washing/drying clothes apply to you, consider this. Based on costs to wash and dry clothes, you'd be paying over $600.00 a year to clean clothes. You could keep that money by saving up to buy your own machines. Or, when looking for an apartment or house to rent, get one that comes with a washer and dryer.

The above budget is based on a household with 2 working adults and up to 4 children. Budgeted expenses are based on items common to a lot of people. This is a sample. It's tight, but it's realistic. If you can budget using the sample amount, you'll be well on your way to better. However, your actual budget will be based on your current total income from all sources, number of working adults, household size, and actual expenses.

Saving was included in the most important monthly bills/expenses because it's important. If you make a budget and take out saving last, you'll always end up not saving. If you pay the most important things first, including saving, you'll make the rest of the money work toward other things. It'll work out. Saving has to be done and seen as important. It has to be top priority. If it's not, it'll be very hard to get out of your current situation. The goal is to get better and move forward.

The more money you put toward saving the better off you'll be. The quicker you save, the quicker you can get to where you want to go. Make sacrifices now for you and your family, in order to have better later on. Everyone will appreciate and benefit from it. Once the goal is reached, you'll be glad to have stuck with the budget.

If you save at least $173.60 per month like listed here, you'll have over $2000.00 at the end of the year, just by saving. Try to increase savings to 10% or 15% each month. If that's too much, stick with the 8% and keep saving. When you get additional money from a tax refund or a side job, add that to your saving. The quicker you save, the quicker you can get to where you want to go. It'll only work if you stick with it, each time.

One way to stay on track is to go old school. Get a box of envelopes. Write the names of bills/expenses and monthly amounts on them. Pay each bill from the envelope. Once the money is gone from an envelope, it's gone. You can't borrow from another envelope. If you do, saving money and bills will get messed up. This will only work if you're willing to trust and follow the process.

Try to have everyone in the home working together with the budget. If everyone is working together to save money for a car, apartment, furniture, etc., it won't take as long. If you can't get everyone to work together, go at it alone. Do your best to move forward. Maybe when you get there, the rest of the family will be motivated to join in.

If you can keep following your budget for 90 days, you'll be able to keep going for a year. During that time, keep remembering why you're on a budget. Keep remembering what you're going after and why. Always remember the why. You'll see progress and will know that goal is within reach.

Teens, unless you usually help with bills at home, this type of budget won't apply to you. However, it can be used as a guide for a current part-time job and later in life.

You don't have to live by a budget all the time, if you're saving a certain amount each month and paying most important bills first. But, it's a good idea to pay attention to how you're spending money. If there's a goal you want to reach, it will be necessary to get back to budgeting. At that time, devote the most money, time, and energy to that goal.

Now that you've gotten important information that will be needed, here are samples of different kind of jobs that you may want to think about applying for.

These are not your dream jobs, like ones mentioned in a previous chapter. These are starter jobs.

Sample starter jobs: Clerk at auto supply stores, Service technician in tire installation departments within department stores, Oil change technician at auto shops, Stock clerk at office supply stores, Cashier at fast food restaurants, Stock clerk, bakery clerk, meat cutter or customer service clerk at grocery stores, Cart master at grocery stores, Restaurant waiter, Personal shopper at department stores, Stock clerk at retail stores, Sales clerk at retail stores, Gas station cashier, Stock clerk or cashier at hardware stores, Desk clerk or member service rep at gyms, Hotel clerk.

Whatever job is chosen, give it your best. You never know where it'll lead to next. The right people always notice. They may not notice right away, but they notice.

This information isn't about how much money you can earn in a lifetime. It's more about the power of making right choices. It's about how it gives the ability to make your life and other people's lives better.

Success isn't just about fancy cars, big houses, and tons of money.

Doing your very best and working hard is success too. Being the first one in the family to own a house or a car is success.

Being the first in the family to get a GED or go to college is success. Being a person of good, positive change is success. Accomplishing things that make you better, happy, or helping other people is success. You have the power to be successful. You have the power.

Definition of daily success – I did my best today. I gave it all that I could. I used all of my ability.

IMPORTANT INFORMATION TO KNOW

- **RESUME'**
  A resume' is a single sheet of neatly typed information that lists your name/contact information, work experience, education, and skills.

- **COVER LETTER**
  A cover letter is a three to four paragraphs letter included with certain job applications. This letter is used to show your interest in the position, why you're applying at that particular company and your top qualifications.

- **PROFESSIONAL REFERENCE**
  A professional reference is a statement given by one of your former supervisors. It's an email, written letter, or phone conversation telling what your duties were while at that company and if you'd be a good candidate for the position you're applying for.

- **PERSONAL REFERENCE**
  A personal reference is a statement telling what type of person you are. It's given by someone you know, such as a friend, teacher, coach, or counselor.

- **BENEFITS**
  Benefits are extra money values most companies offer full time employees. The extras may include paid vacations, paid insurance, paid holidays, paid sick days, paid personal days, education benefits. Some benefits start at first day of hire, others begin after a waiting period. Full type of benefits offered depends on the company.

IMPORTANT INFORMATION TO KNOW

- **TEMPORARY EMPLOYEE**
  A temporary employee is someone a company hires for a limited amount of time. The worker may be hired for one day, a week, several months, or even a year. Companies hire employees directly or through a temporary agency. Temporary workers aren't eligible to receive benefits. Most are paid weekly.

- **FULL TIME EMPLOYEE**
  A full-time employee is someone who may work between 30 – 40 hours per week. The actual hours considered full time are determined by the company and explained or given to employees when hired.

- **OVERTIME PAY**
  Overtime pay is the rate paid to an employee who has worked beyond his full-time work week hours. It's also referred to as time and a half. Example. An employee who is paid $12.00 per hour is paid $18.00 per hour for any hour worked past his 30 – 40 hour full time work week
  ($12.00 +1/2 of 12.00 = $18.00)

- **PART TIME EMPLOYEE**
  A part time employee is an employee working any hours less than the companies' stated full time employee hours. Part time employees could work a few hours or days in a week.

- **SEASONAL EMPLOYEE**
  A seasonal employee is someone hired to work during holidays or special events.

FOR A SUCCESSFUL JOB SEARCH

- Look For a Job Online Through Job Search Sites Like Indeed.com, Monster.com, Snag A Job.com, Simply Hired.com, or on Company Sites That You're Interested in

- Let Other People Know You're Looking For Work. Maybe They Know Who's Hiring or Know of Someone Who Will Give You a Start

- Apply Everyday

- Fill Out Several Applications a Day

- Practice Answering Interview Questions (See Sample Interview Questions in this Chapter)

- Stay Hopeful

- Don't Give Up

COMMON INTERVIEW QUESTIONS

1. Why do you want to work here?

2. What are your strengths?

3. What are your weaknesses?

4. Why should I hire you?

5. What are some ways people would describe you?

6. Where/How do you see yourself in 5 years?

These are just a few common questions. Interviewers may ask some or all of these. Expect to be asked more or similar questions like these. (See sample answers in this chapter)

DAY BEFORE INTERVIEW

- Know the Time and Place of the Interview

- Know Type of Business or Company You're Applying to

- Know How You Can Benefit the Company By Working There

- Know Why You Want to Work for the Company

- Have Everything Ready That You'll Need to Get Out the Door on Time

- Arrange for a Friend or Someone You Trust to Watch Your Kids During Your Interview

DAY OF INTERVIEW

- Dress Appropriately

- Go Alone

- Be on Time or a Few Minutes Early

- Turn Off Cellphone a Few Minutes Before Interview

- Be Enthusiastic. Show That You Want to Work

- Be Respectful

- Answer Questions Clearly and Honestly

- Speak Positively

- Maintain Eye Contact

- Keep Your Attention on the Interviewer and Questions Being Asked

- Tell Interviewer Why You're the Best Person for the Job

- Show Interest in the Job by Paying Attention and Asking Questions

- Smile. It Will Help You to Relax and Also Show That You're Friendly

- Shake the Interviewer's Hand After the Interview

TIPS FOR A GOOD JOB EXPERIENCE

- Be On Time

- Show Up Each Day That You're Scheduled to Work

- Do the Job Right and Work Hard

- Do Your Very Best Each Day

- Get Along With People You're Working With

- Treat Co-Workers and Customers How You Want to Be Treated

- Listen and Follow Supervisor's Instructions

- Control Your Mouth and Temper

- Respect Yourself, Co-Workers, and Customers

- Work With Co-Workers and Get the Job Done

REASONS PEOPLE MAY LOSE JOBS

- Not Showing Up for Work When Scheduled

- Always Late

- Not Getting Along With Co-Workers

- Taking Too Many Breaks or Overstaying Breaks

- Constantly Using Personal Cellphone or Texting While Working

- Missing Too Many Days

- Playing Around Instead of Working

- Arguing/Fighting With Co-Workers or Customers

- Not Following Company Rules

- Poor Work Quality

- Sleeping on the Job

GETTING TO SUPERVISOR LEVEL

- Lisen to and Follow Supervisor's Instructions

- Be Nice and Helpful

- Listen. Watch. Learn From Your Supervisor

- Have and Keep a Good Attitude

- Do Quality Work

- Care About Doing a Good Job

- Be Willing to Train for Other Positions

- Provide Excellent Customer Service

- Get Along With Co-Workers

- Prevent and/or Solve Problems

- Value Customers

WINNING CUSTOMER SERVICE

- Treat All Customers With Respect

- Be Patient With Customers

- See Customers as Important

- Respectfully Address Customers By Ma'am, Miss, or Sir

- Acknowledge Walk-in or Walk-up Customers When Helping Another Customer. This Could Easily Be Done By Looking at the Person and Saying One Minute Please

- Communicate With Customers When a Service is Delayed

- Thank Customers

- Avoid Having Customers Wait Too Long

- Listen to Customer's Concerns and Try to Solve the Problem

- Stay Professional in Tone of Voice, Actions, and Attitude

- Be Helpful and Friendly

CHAPTER SIX

You're Stronger Than You Think

Deciding to choose better and making it happen takes courage and strength. You should give yourself a pat on the back for stepping up to do it. If you keep working hard, many good changes will come.

To get to that place, another kind of strength and toughness will have to be shown. You will have to be able to control your actions and reactions. Using self-control will help make better life choices and keep you moving toward better.

One thing that we always have control over is us. We have control over how we act, react, and do things. In our hands, we hold the ability to change outcomes, just by making good decisions and keeping cool.

Don't let your temper run wild. Tame it. You have the power to choose words and how you say them. You live with choices made, good or bad. The next time you find yourself getting angry, ask yourself if that thing is worth getting upset over.

When we don't stop ourselves from saying or doing the wrong things, we can quickly regret it. We have control over what we do and that influences how our lives turn out. Big and little things will happen, so we have to stay focused. How we react to a challenge is what impacts the outcome.

Keep negativity out. Don't let people or circumstances steal progress made. If that happens, you won't see how far you can really go. You won't see how much talent there is inside.

Don't let people trap you into an argument or fight. Recognize it as a distraction. Angry words can add stress and take a simple situation to a higher level or even a dangerous one.

When someone is rude or disrespectful towards us it's easy to respond the same way. It's easy to think, *they're disrespecting me. I'm going to get them straight. I'm going to show them I'm not weak.* Can I tell you this? Don't go there. Don't go to their level.

You're tough and can take on the best of them. But, you have nothing to prove. You're stronger than you think. Focus on what's most important. Instead of arguing, a better approach would be to show your real strength. It doesn't take strength or effort to tell someone off. Anybody can do that. You're strongest when you control yourself. That takes effort, thought, and strength. Even if you tell them off, other people who are the same way will show up, somewhere else.

If cursing, name calling, or yelling comes into the picture, the situation will get worse. You may be reading this and saying to yourself that you can't help it. That's how you are. It's what you have always done. During those times, you were choosing to react those ways. You can change how you respond. It's really a choice.

I'm not saying to let people walk all over you. What I'm saying is, think about how the wrong reaction will affect tomorrow, the day after that, and the next one. You're looking at just that moment. You've been working too hard for a better future to mess it up. See how it will affect that good future.

Everyone has stress. Everybody has to deal with it. Keeping our cool doesn't just happen. We have to make the decision to do it. We have to choose to do it, each time something happens. If the urge comes to set someone straight, give these suggestions a try. Take a deep breath or two or three. Walk away. Or, if you're in an area where you can't leave, try this. Before responding to the person, under your breath, start counting backwards, 100 to zero. Counting backwards buys time for you to gain control of yourself. It helps to calm down. It'll also help you to think of better ways to handle situations. Stick with these tips and you will see improvements and better outcomes.

Think about it. Has your way been making situations better? The answer is likely no. Try it out. Give it a chance. If you keep doing it, it'll become a habit. You will find a better, calmer way to handle situations. Some weight of stress will be lifted. Wouldn't that be nice?

Also, consider this.

Two men were in a parking lot arguing. A teenage boy of one of the men stood watching. Suddenly, the dad stopped yelling and got quiet. The other man kept shouting. After everything was over and the man left, the boy asked his dad a question. Angry and confused, he asked, "Pops, why did you stand there and let that man talk to you like that?"

Putting an arm around his son's shoulder, he said, "Son, at first, I was so mad, I couldn't see straight. But, I needed to solve the problem. Getting quiet gave me time to calm down and think of a solution. A mad man can't think."

It takes practice. When in an angry situation, stay calm. Try to come up with a good solution. Come up with a solution that reminds that the good changes made are worth staying calm. As improvements in self-control are made, situations and people won't be so upsetting. You'll get along easier with people and make better decisions. You may even enjoy life more.

Older brothers, those changes can help with being a better example for your younger brothers, cousins, friends, and people around you. Maybe seeing the positive changes in you will move them to make their own better changes.

Dads, improvements aren't just being made for you, but for your children and family too. When they see how well you're handling yourself, it'll help them too.

These are just a few small ways to help. If you find yourself really struggling in this area and suggestions aren't helping, people trained in anger management can help.

Practicing self-control will help in every area of your life. You're stronger than you think. You have it within you. Each day, you have to pull it up and use it. Keep pulling it up. You have strength to do it.

Stick with it, good changes will come. You will see yourself differently. People will see you differently too. They'll see you with eyes of respect.

CHAPTER SEVEN

Fresh Start

Perhaps you're reading this book and can't see yourself in any of the positive outcomes, because you made poor choices. There's still hope for you, if you want it. It's never too late to make yourself better.

Jamal, (not his real name), an 11 year old, lived with his parents and sisters. His mom and dad fought almost every day. Most mornings his dad was drinking and hollerin' and cursin'. When his parents divorced, his dad disappeared from their lives.

In high school, Jamal began fighting and getting in trouble. He listened to voices of people who were making poor choices, doing bad things. He was quickly pulled in by the promise of fast, easy money. Doing bad things soon became normal for him. Police were always knocking on his mom's door. It kept him looking over his shoulder.

Years later, he was sent to prison for 10 years. It caught him off guard. All the other stuff he'd done never got him locked up. When released, he got himself together, with support and help from his mom, a court ordered counselor, and prayer.

He never talked about what went on in jail. But, whatever happened, it kept him saying, he wasn't going back there.

Finding a job seemed impossible. No one wanted to hire him. After a long search, a restaurant finally gave him a chance.

He started working in their kitchen. Later, he moved on to hotel kitchens, where he learned about food and cooking. After that, he found construction jobs. Years later, he ended up getting a contractor's license.

In between years, he reconnected with his children and stayed in their lives. He got married and had more kids. Early on, he started talking to them about doing good in school. They were only 7 and 9 when he started telling them to stay out of trouble. Jail was no joke. It wasn't where they wanted to be.

Today, he's doing a good job of taking care of his family. One of his boys is in college and the other one is on his way. And he has a good relationship with all of his children.

Jamal and other people like him have accepted responsibility for poor choices and sincerely turned their lives around. You can turn your life around too. If you've ever experienced some or all things mentioned here or have had a similar experience, and want to turn your life around, you can.

If you want to change, start by accepting responsibility for your actions. Own them. Admit that you made those poor decisions. Decide to learn from them, by not repeating them. Make better choices. Make decisions that will help you to be and do better. You will have to work hard at change. If you're willing to do your very best and put in the time and work, you can turn your life around.

That change can begin by making better decisions and creating new habits. Get out of the old way of doing things. If you don't have a high school education, get your GED.

If you're a high school graduate, use information in this book to get a job. Hang around people who can help you change for better.

There are places and people who are willing to give you a second chance. Some provide job training and some will also pay you while in training. If you sincerely want to start over, there are people who can help. They can also connect you to places for GED classes, job search, tutoring, counseling, and other resources. All are free. Contact information for some places like that is included in this book.

If there are people who need to hear that you're sincerely sorry, tell them. Ask for their forgiveness. Sincerely ask God to forgive you too. If you're sincere, he'll do it. Ask God to help you. He gives new life. He changes people. Ask God to come into your life and save you. Then find a good church and start going there. Many neighborhood churches are available to choose from. Get and keep a personal relationship with God. You can't make lasting change in your own strength.

You need to forgive too. If you grew up without your dad or mom being in your life, and you're angry about it, you need to forgive. When you choose to forgive, you're not excusing or saying what your dad or mom did was right.

You're not excusing the behavior. You're choosing to help yourself. You're helping yourself move forward. Forgiveness isn't always easy, but it's freeing. It takes away the stress and worry from trying to figure out why.

When we forgive people who have done things that caused us pain, we're helping ourselves. It helps us to start healing emotional wounds. It stops us from being mad at the world. It helps us to move to better.

It allows us to make better choices. It helps us to make good choices for us and the people around us.

We also forgive so that God can forgive us. If we want his forgiveness, we have to forgive others. Don't let unforgiveness hold you back. It may be hard to do, but it'll help you. Start the process. Start letting it go. Forgive and prepare to look ahead.

Whatever you were missing from not having a relationship with your parent, choose different for yourself.

Dads, consider this. Little things like telling your children to do well in school, saying *good job,* saying *I'm proud of you* go a long way. Taking your kids to a park and watching them run around is time well spent. Taking them to a fast food restaurant or to buy something small from a store each month will give them something nice to look forward to. Not only will you be spending time together, but you'd be making good, lasting memories.

CHAPTER EIGHT
Looking Ahead

You have all the information needed right here to get started on the road to success. It'll only work if you'll roll up your sleeves and do it. Take this information and run with it. Take full advantage of it. Make it work for you. Become all that you can be. Give it your all.

Stay motivated and encouraged. Keep growing. Keep learning. There will be many lessons along the way. Don't see them as hard moments. Learn from them. See them as teachable moments. If you get discouraged, don't quit. Remember progress made and keep going. Just because something doesn't work out one way doesn't mean it can't be done another way and be successful. Just keep trying. Do the work and stay on track. Do your best. You will make it.

I'm very thankful for all the people who God has sent to help me along the way. If it weren't for Him and each of them, I wouldn't have been able to write this book. Just like me, there were many people who God sent to help you along the way. You probably didn't notice, but they were there all along. They were investing in you and your future.

That single dad or mom who dropped out of school, but made sure you got an education, helped. That aunt and uncle who made sure you went to church, even when they weren't going, helped.

That grandma or grandpa who stood at the front of the church asking the pastor and church to keep you in prayer helped.

People who always gave you a ride to work helped. People who watched your kids while you were working helped. People who took the time to give a personal reference so that you'd get a job helped. That pastor who kept asking about your grades and checking on you at school helped. That brother, sister, or cousin, who made sure you stayed out of trouble helped.

There will be many more people helping along the way. Remember them too. You may be the one doing all the work to get where you're going, but you won't be getting there alone. There will be people helping you just because they see you trying to do better.

If you end up with your own business, there will be people supporting you just because they want to help businesses like yours. There will be college students and retired men and women volunteering to prepare you for the GED test. There will be non-profit businesses giving their time and helping with many resources.

What's my point? You were being set up for better all along. It's still going on. God didn't forget about you. Now that you see it, be thankful. Do something that will make all of those people proud. Do something that you'd be pleased with too.

Build your future. Achieve. Be the first in your family to get a good job. Be the first to work hard and buy a car. Be the first to work hard and get a GED. Be the first to go to college. Be the first to own a business. Whatever that first is for you, be that first. But, don't be the last.

Bring the rest along. Pull people forward. While you're learning and getting better, reach back and help someone else. Help other people win. Help them be successful too. Helping others is just as important as receiving help. Help your family members, but don't stop there. Extend your reach to that next-door neighbor.

Stretch hands to people across the street and around the corner. You have the ability to change your neighborhood, just by helping others. You even have the ability to change your city. It starts with just one person. You could be that person.

After you make it, don't be afraid to help other people then too. You won't lose what you already have by helping someone else. You'll gain so much more. There's enough success to go around for everyone. It's available to anyone willing to put in the time and hard work.

If after receiving your help other people end up having more than you, be happy for them. Take time to tell them congratulations man! They may have had to overcome more situations and obstacles than you. They learned from you and other people and were able to go to a new level. You were a part of that and helped with making their lives better. That's a good thing.

When someone ends up with more than you, it doesn't take away what you already have. You don't lose what you already have. You still have yours. See the possibilities in helping each other. Their product, service, or business could end up helping you, your mama, daddy, sisters, brothers, grandma, your children, friends, and entire neighborhood. See the possibilities.

Maybe they'll open businesses that would provide jobs for your family. Maybe those same businesses would be what people in your neighborhood want or need. They could open affordable daycare centers, laundromats, bakeries, doctor's offices, dentist offices, barbershops, gyms, grocery stores, restaurants, or insurance companies.

Instead of being upset because they have more, take time to learn from them. Gaining that knowledge could get you to the next or their level. It'd be a win/win for everyone. You helped them and they won. Learn from them and you'll win.

Challenge. Take time to help at least five people. That's a very small number considering there are millions of people in the world. It's a great, manageable start. You don't have to make a big announcement about it. Just do it. Ask those five people to help at least five other people.

Make part of your help service. You may even discover it's a wonderful thing to help somebody else. When you can, donate to those non-profit companies that helped you or your family. Some of those businesses were started by people who came from the same situations as you and dedicate their time to helping others.

Donate to that neighborhood church or ministry that helped you or family stay on the right track. Don't just donate money, donate your time too. Teach a business or music class. Organize and run a sports team. Be a mentor. Teach a health and wellness class. Be a tutor. Give cooking classes. Start an arts program.

Donate your skills and talents. Show someone else how to be and do better. Use all that you've learned. Use all that you will learn. Use your talents to show other people a way up!

CONCLUSION

One final thought I'd like to leave with you is this. The only person you're destined to be is the person you decide to be. Keep a picture of what you want to be in front of you.

Slow and steady wins the race, but it doesn't have to take a lifetime to get there. What you do during the slower times determines how quickly you get there. Don't quit.

Keep doing something every day. You will see a change for the better. You will see your dream and better come to pass. Keep going and moving forward. Keep doing the right things. Keep making good choices.

I hope you'll see this as only the beginning. Make the decision that you're going to stay focused. Be determined to walk into a better life.

Think about reaching your goal, dream, or better, like being in a race. Suppose you're close enough to the finish line to see it, but you're really tired. At that moment, you could do one of two things. You could keep thinking about being too tired and then stop and quit. Or, you could see all the other runners crossing the finish line and decide that you're going to cross the finish line with them. If you decide to quit, it would be hard living with the regret of being that close and giving up.

To get to the finish line, keep your eyes on the reward. Keep seeing what it'll be like when the end is reached. Keep going when you don't feel like it or when it gets hard.

Many people before you made it, you can too. Pull you forward. Start and end days with good. Speak positive words about you and your future.

See and make each day better. Start each day with hope. It'll change you on the inside and help you get to the end of your dream, goal, and new beginning.

Little by little, step by step, you'll gain bold confidence. You'll know that you're going to finish what you started. One day you'll look back and say, *I made it.* You'll be glad that you kept going and didn't give up.

Going after your dream and better will take discipline and courage. If you consistently work toward those things, you'll get there. At times, you won't be able to make some of the improvements and changes in your own strength. God could help with that. If you know God or get to know him later, get him involved. He could help you do what you can't.

If you run into issues or just need someone to listen, you could talk to Him. He is someone you can go to 24/7. He's someone you can call friend. He's someone you can call your own. He'd listen and help. He'd help because he loves you. God is kind and merciful. The Lord is bigger than any problem. He specializes in the impossible.

ADDITIONAL JOB, RESOURCES, AND EDUCATION HELP

Businesses on this page help youths who have dropped out of school and are out of work. They provide **paid and unpaid job training/services** in the hotel industry, restaurant industry, construction, and other areas. **Please check company websites for full, updated information, age requirements, qualifications, and additional resources.**

<u>New Orleans Area Residents Only</u>
Liberty's Kitchen
Liberty's Kitchen Youth Development Program
To learn more, email ydp@libertyskitchen.org
or go to their website, www.libertyskitchen.org
(504) 822-4011

Café Reconcile
**Café Reconcile Strive Future Leaders Program
(Only assists youth and young adults currently or previously involved with the juvenile or adult legal system)**
To learn more, contact grow@cafereconcile.org
or go to their website, www.cafereconcile.org
(504) 568-1157

YEP (Youth Empowerment Project)
YEP Works Program
To learn more, contact info@youthempowermentproject.org
Or go to their website, www.youthempowermentproject.org
(504) 522-1316

YEP (Youth Empowerment Project)
Care Center
Hahnville, LA
(985) 331-3032

Louisiana Green Corps (LAGC)
To learn more, contact info@lagreencorps.org
or go to their website, www.lagreencorps.org
(504) 613-4661

Louisiana Job Support Services

Goodwill Industries
New Orleans, Louisiana
Goodwill's Re-Integration Program
(Re-Entry Job Skills Training)
(**Available to eligible participants who were released from the Louisiana Dept. of Corrections, Federal Prison System or City/Parish prison within the last 7 years**)
Visit their website for more information,
www.goodwillno.org
(504) 456-2622

Goodwill Industries
New Orleans, Louisiana
Goodwill Education Advancement & Readiness (GEAR) Program
(Job Readiness Training Program)
For more information, go to their website at
www.goodwillno.org
(504) 889-5553

JOB1 New Orleans Louisiana
New Orleans, Louisiana
Free job search and placement help, career counseling, and resume' writing.
For more information go to their website, www.job1nola.org
(504) 658-4500

Volunteers of America Southeast Louisiana
New Orleans, Louisiana
Positive Pathways Program
Connects at-risk and justice system involved youth to educational programs and job training. For more information call (504) 836-8701
Visit their website,
www.voasela.org/services/children-and-family-services

Louisiana Job Support Services Continued

Baton Rouge Regional Library Career Center
7711 Goodwood Blvd.
Baton Rouge, LA
Free interview practice, job application assistance, computer use, job information videos, and career coaching
(225) 231-3733

National Job Support Services

Salvation Army
Salvation Army Hands up Employment Services and Support Services
Job-search counseling, support, and programs that teach new job skills.
Go to their website, www.salvationarmyusa.org
(Search by your State)

Free Career and Technical Training

New Orleans Louisiana Only - Orleans Parish Residents Only

New Orleans Career Center
New Orleans, LA 70116
New Orleans Career Center offers free training to all public high school students and adults 18 or older with a high school diploma or GED.
Training is only available to Orleans Parish residents.
Free training is offered in the following areas:
Healthcare, Building Trades, Engineering, Manufacturing, Culinary Arts, and Information Technology.
For complete information and to learn more, go to their website, www.nolacc.org or call (504) 372-1502.

Free GED Classes

Louisiana Residents Only

YEP (Youth Empowerment Project)
YEP Educates
(Available to out of school youths ages 16 and up)
To learn more, go to their website
www.youthempowermentproject.org

YEP Educates Locations:
YEP Educates - Mid City
Adult Learning Center
139 South Broad St.
New Orleans, LA 70119
504-658-9221

YEP Educates - West Bank
Arthur Monday Center
1111 Newton St.
Algiers, LA 70114
504-658-4577

New Orleans East:
12000 Hayne Blvd.,
New Orleans, LA 70128
(504) 400-9872

YMCA of Greater New Orleans
YMCA Educational Services (YES)
New Orleans, LA
Classes are held at Main library, by appointment only
Call for an appointment and requirements, (504) 596-3842

Free GED Classes Continued

Louisiana Residents Only

Volunteer Instructors Teaching Adults (VITA)
For more information go to their website, www.vitalaf.org
(337) 234-4600 Lafayette, LA
(337) 942-1511 Opelousas, LA

Christa McAuliffe Adult Learning Center
12000 Goodwood Blvd.
Baton Rouge, LA
For more information, class hours, and to pre-register call
(225) 226-7631

Texas Residents Only
Dallas Public Library
In-person classes are available at various locations, with no limit to the number of classes allowed to take.
For more information contact adultlearning@dallas.gov
Or go to website for updates, www.dallaslibrary2.org
(214) 671-8291 – Adult Learning Team

Important note – all GED classes are open to adults 18 and older, unless noted. By law, in all states, everyone under 18 must attend school. If you're under 18 and dropped out of school, you'll have to get approval to take GED classes. Agencies that help out-of-school youths can help with getting paperwork and approval. If you're not involved in any youth agencies, written permission will be needed from your parent or guardian. You must also get a waiver form, paper work, and age requirements from the principal at your last school attended.

To find free GED classes in your state, look up free adult literacy programs or classes.

Free Adult Reading Classes

Louisiana Residents
YMCA
YMCA Educational Services (YES)
Adult Family Literacy
They provide reading tutoring in New Orleans, Jefferson, St. Charles, St. John parishes.
Call for information, (504) 596-3842

Adult Literacy Advocates of Greater Baton Rouge
7732 Goodwood Blvd.
Baton Rouge, LA 70806
They provide in-person reading tutoring for adults 18 and older.
For more information, go to their website,
www.adultliteracyadvocates.org
Call to make an appointment, (225) 383-1090

Free Homework Help
Louisiana Residents Only

www.homeworkLA.org
Live one-to-one homework help with expert tutors. Tutors are available 7 days a week,
2:00 p.m. – midnight

Tutors help:
- Students up to 12th grade
- Early college students
- Adult learners

Tutors help with:
- Homework questions in math, science, English, social studies, and writing
- Test Prep and SAT
- GED practice quizzes

Free Homework Help
Alabama Residents Only

www.homeworkalabama.org
Live one-to-one homework help with expert tutors. Tutors are available 7 days a week,
10:00 a.m. – 11:00 p.m.

Tutors help:
- Students K - 12th grade
- College students
- Adult learners

Some Available Resources:
- Self-study & Test prep tools
- Math & English video lessons
- AP® Video Lessons
- SAT®/ACT® Essentials

To find free homework help in your state, go online and search free homework help plus your state.

IMPORTANT COLLEGE INFORMATION

Postsecondary Education
The education level that follows the successful completion of high school. It involves enrollment in a university, college, or vocational school.

Major
The field a college student will be studying, such as business, accounting, or engineering.

College Credits
Amounts of hours spent in class. Most single-semester college courses are worth three credits.

Tuition
Costs students pay to attend college.

Vocational/Technical School or College
Provides instructional programs or courses that focus on skills needed for a particular job function. Students receive hands-on, job specific training and receive certification upon completion of a program. Programs usually last less than 6 months or up to one year.

Associate Degree
A two-year college degree that can be obtained from a community or junior college.

Bachelor's Degree
A four-year college degree that can be obtained from a college or university.

Master's Degree
Additional study up to two years following a Bachelor's degree.

WAYS TO PAY FOR COLLEGE

Federal Pell Grants

Federal Pell Grants are grants that help pay for the cost of college. Full and partial grant amounts are awarded to undergraduate students who show exceptional financial need and haven't earned a bachelor's, graduate, or professional degree. It's best to apply early.

To apply, submit your Free Application for Federal Student Aid (FAFSA®) form. If you meet the basic eligibility criteria for federal student aid, the financial aid office at your college determines how much free aid you are eligible to receive.

Federal Work-Study

Federal Work-Study allows undergraduate and graduate students with financial need to work part-time jobs on or off campus, while enrolled in college.

Federal Work Study is available to full-time or part-time students. It's administered by schools participating in the Federal Work-Study Program. Check with your school's financial aid office to find out if your school participates. Funds are limited, so you must apply early.

Scholly Search® (Free search App to find free full and partial scholarships)

United Negro College Fund

WAYS TO PAY FOR COLLEGE

Federal Loans

Federal student loans are made by the government, with terms and conditions that are set by law. They have fixed interest rates.

Private Loans

Private loans are made by private organizations such as banks, credit unions, and state-based or state-affiliated organizations, and have terms and conditions that are set by the lender. They're usually more expensive than federal student loans.

Louisiana Residents Only

GO Grant

The Louisiana GO Grant assists students who can show financial need to pay for the cost of college. The GO Grant is used to pay a portion of the cost of attendance at an eligible Louisiana postsecondary institution. To be eligible for Louisiana GO Grant, a student must:

- Be a Louisiana Resident;
- File a Free Application for Federal Student Aid (FAFSA);
- Receive a Federal Pell grant;
- Have remaining financial need after deducting Estimated Family Contribution (EFC) and all federal/state/institutional grant or scholarship aid ("gift aid") from student's cost of attendance;
- Be a student enrolled at least half-time

Through Free Application For Federal Student Aid (FAFSA), You can apply for Pell Grants, Work Study Program, Go Grants, and Federal Loans. - Free Application for Federal Student Aid, www.fafsa.ed.gov

WAYS TO PAY FOR COLLEGE

Visit these sites for additional financial aid information

La. Office of Student Financial Assistance
www.mylosfa.la.gov

www.Studentaid.gov

SOME COLLEGES/UNIVERSITIES

ALABAMA

- Alabama A&M University
- Alabama State University
- Bishop State Community College
- Concordia College Selma
- Gadsden State Community College
- F. Drake Technical College
- Lawson State Community College
- Miles College
- Oakwood University
- Selma University
- Shelton State Community College
- Stillman College
- Talladega College
- Trenholm State Technical College
- Tuskegee University

ARKANSAS

- Arkansas Baptist College
- Philander Smith College
- Shorter College
- University of Arkansas at Pine Bluff

DISTRICT OF COLUMBIA

- Howard University
- University of the District of Columbia

FLORIDA

- Bethune-Cookman University
- Edward Waters University
- Florida A&M University
- Florida A&M University College of Law
- Florida Memorial University

SOME COLLEGES/UNIVERSITIES

GEORGIA

- Albany State University
- Clark Atlanta University
- Fort Valley State University
- Interdenominational Theological Center
- Morehouse College
- Morehouse School of Medicine
- Morris Brown College
- Paine College
- Savannah State University

LOUISIANA

- Dillard University
- Grambling State University
- Southern University
- Southern University Law Center
- Xavier University of Louisiana

MARYLAND

- Bowie State University
- Coppin State University
- Morgan State University
- University of Maryland, Eastern Shore

MISSISSIPPI

- Alcorn State University
- Jackson State University
- Mississippi Valley State University
- Rust College
- Tougaloo College

SOME COLLEGES/UNIVERSITIES

NORTH CAROLINA

- Barber-Scotia College
- Elizabeth City State University
- Fayetteville State University
- Johnson C. Smith University
- Livingstone College
- North Carolina A&T State University
- North Carolina Central University
- St. Augustine's University
- Shaw University
- Winston Salem State University

OHIO

- Central State University
- Wilberforce University

SOUTH CAROLINA

- Allen University
- Benedict College
- Claflin University
- Clinton College
- Denmark Technical College
- Morris College
- South Carolina State University
- Voorhees College

SOME COLLEGES/UNIVERSITIES

TENNESSEE

- American Baptist College
- Fisk University
- Knoxville College
- Lane College
- LeMoyne-Owen College
- Meharry Medical College
- Tennessee State University

TEXAS

- Huston-Tillotson University
- Jarvis Christian College
- Paul Quinn College
- Prairie View A&M University
- Saint Philip's College
- Southwestern Christian College
- Texas College
- Texas Southern University
- TSU Thurgood Marshall School of Law
- Wiley College

SUGGESTED READING

A Hand to Guide Me
Denzel Washington

The Power of Broke
Daymond John

NOTE: These books may be found in libraries. If they're not in a library near you, make a book add request through a local library website or library staff.

SUGGESTED LISTENING

T.D. Jakes Ministries
All social media platforms

Ralph Douglas West Ministries
The Church without Walls
All social media platforms

Joel Osteen Ministries
All social media platforms

GOD CARES ABOUT YOU

Jesus will never reject you. He won't give up on you, even if you've given up on yourself. God has high hopes for you. He often thinks about you and sees you as valuable.

I believe a fresh start begins with Jesus. Real lasting change comes from having a personal relationship with God. Jesus is the only true hope and one who can fill the emptiness that's within us. I believe having a personal relationship with the Lord fills that emptiness.

If you don't know Jesus and want to have true happiness and peace, I encourage you to pray the prayer below. As you say these words and believe with your heart, you will be born again.

Father God, I need you. Take control of my life. Jesus, I believe you are the Son of God. I believe you died on the cross for me and rose from the dead. I ask you to come into my heart and life. I receive you as my Savior and Lord, turning away from my sins and placing my trust in you. Thank you for forgiving my sins and saving me. I pray this in Jesus' name. Amen.

If you sincerely prayed this prayer, you're now saved. You're born again. You're forgiven and cleansed from all sins. I John 1:9

With that simple prayer, you can get and keep life-long happiness, peace, and a personal relationship with God. Read the Bible daily and follow God's laws. Pray daily and attend a good Bible-based church to receive encouragement and more of God's Word.

That if thou shalt confess with thy mouth the Lord Jesus, and shalt believe in thine heart that God hath raised Him from the dead, thou shalt be saved. Romans 10:9 - 10

Visit these retailers for Angie Dent's books:

www.Amazon.com

www.Avidbookshop.com

www.barnesandnoble.com

www.booksamillion.com

www.cavalierhousebooks.com

www.eshaverbooks.com

www.gardendistrictbookshop.com

www.hudsonbooksellers.com

www.malaprops.com

www.octaviabooks.com

www.passbooksonline.com

www.politics-prose.com

www.parnassusbooks.net

www.regulatorbookshop.com

www.scuppernongbooks.com

www.squarebooks.com

Be the first to know when Angie Dent's next book is available! To get an alert whenever she has a new release, preorder or discount:

Follow her at
https://www.bookbub.com/authors/angie-dent

or click +Follow button at
https://www.amazon.com./author/angiedent

Follow on Twitter: @AuthoraAngie

About the Author

Angie Dent is a former youth mentor. She's a Christian author who writes books to give people hope and peace of mind.

Angie began writing over 10 years ago and has won several awards through the Louisiana State Poetry Society and Fleur de Lis Poetry Society.

Made in the USA
Columbia, SC
02 July 2024

38026568R00072